the
Scott...
Quiz
Book

the Scottish Quiz Book

WAVERLEY
BOOKS

This new edition published 2010 by Waverley Books Ltd
144 Port Dundas Road, Glasgow G4 0HZ, Scotland

First published 2002 by Geddes & Grosset
Revised and updated 2006

New edition © 2010 Waverley Books Ltd

ISBN 978 1 84934 030 4

Printed and bound in the UK

Contents

Answers

QUESTIONS

General Knowledge 1

1   Where is the Queen's View?
2   How many Scottish members sat in parliament after the Act of Union in 1707?
3   In which century did Balmoral Castle come into the possession of the royal family?
4   Which ruined Scottish castle is said to have inspired Bram Stoker?
5   Where is the Scottish Lead Mining museum?
6   What was the profession of John Kibble, who erected the Kibble Palace in Glasgow?
7   With which Scottish island is the name of the author Gavin Maxwell associated?
8   What was manufactured by J. & P. Coats?
9   Some people believe that Pontius Pilate was born in Scotland. Where is he said to have been born?
10 Where are the Falls of Braan?
11 In which city is the Rosemount Viaduct?
12 What is the name of the steam railway that operates out of Aviemore?
13 Why does the earth move in the village of Comrie?
14 What is the Lanthorn of the North?
15 Near which village on the north coast is Smoo Cave?
16 Where is Flora MacDonald buried?
17 Which Scottish builder was known as 'Concrete Bob'?
18 Which building in Haddington is known as 'the Lamp of the Lothians'?
19 What was the name of the medieval murder-mystery film in which Sean Connery starred in 1986?
20 What was the name of the world's first paddle-steamer, built on the Clyde in 1812?
21 Which famous Scottish painter lived in Howden House in Livingston?
22 Near which town in Dumfries and Galloway is the Motte of Ur?
23 Which famous Scottish writer is buried at Dryburgh Abbey?
24 In which Scottish castle did Madonna and Guy Ritchie tie the knot?
25 Where in Scotland will you find Europe's largest onshore wind farm?

Answers: p133

Industry 1

1 What was Scotland's most important export in the mid-eighteenth century?
2 Which two Scottish cities were centres of the whaling industry in Scotland?
3 Which city was once the biggest tobacco trading port in Great Britain?
4 What was the dominant textile industry in the first half of the nineteenth century in Scotland?
5 Where on mainland Scotland is the centre of the whisky distilling industry?
6 What part of Scotland is famous for its commercial soft fruit growing?
7 Where did whisky blender Johnny Walker first set up shop?
8 In which town in Scotland was George Sandeman (of Sandeman's Port) born?
9 Which two names in whisky are associated with Perth?
10 What was the name of the Scottish grocer who made his name and fortune in the tea trade in the nineteenth century?
11 In which village in Scotland was the Bonawe Iron Furnace?
12 Which company pioneered the brewing of lager in Scotland?
13 What was produced at the Dens Works in Dundee?
14 Where is the head office of the Baxters Food Group?
15 What was the Camperdown Works?
16 Where was Singer's sewing machine factory based in Scotland?
17 In which year did the Ravenscraig Steelworks open?
18 Where was the Seafield Colliery?
19 Which two industries were based at Prestonpans?
20 Where in central Scotland was the shale-oil industry based?
21 When was Ravenscraig finally closed down?
22 When did the car plant at Linwood open?
23 What is the Saltire Prize which was launched in December 2008 by the Scottish government?
24 What were the St Rollox Works?
25 In which city was the Timex factory?

Answers: p133

Food & Drink 1

1   What is the main ingredient of cullen skink?
2   What is crowdie?
3   What is traditionally used as the casing for haggis?
4   What food product is Arbroath famous for?
5   Which Scottish town is famous for its bridies?
6   What is traditionally eaten with haggis on Burns Night?
7   What other ingredient is put in Scotch broth apart from vegetables and stock?
8   What kind of meat is used for making potted haugh?
9   What is a Selkirk bannock?
10 When is black bun traditionally served?
11 What beverage is produced at Traquair?
12 What is thought to give malt whisky its distinctive flavour?
13 What was a mutchkin?
14 What gave the Fountainbridge area in Edinburgh its distinctive smell?
15 What are 'silver darlings'?
16 What are the ingredients of Atholl brose?
17 What is 'gundy'?
18 What does *uisge-beatha* mean?
19 What is a Jethart Snail?
20 What are stovies?
21 What is the main ingredient of partan bree?
22 What dish is made with oatmeal, cream and raspberries?
23 From which part of Scotland does Dunlop cheese originate?
24 Which breed of cattle has given Scottish beef an international reputation for quality?
25 What is traditionally sprinkled on porridge before it is eaten?

Answers: p134

QUESTIONS

Television Trivia

1   What is the name of the fictional area of Glasgow in BBC Scotland's soap, *River City*?

2   Which television comedy show spawned the catchphrase 'Gonnae no dae that?'?

3   Which Scottish chef and television personality has starred in both the UK and the US series of *Hell's Kitchen*?

4   Name the Scotsman who starred in *One Foot in the Grave*.

5   What was the name of the lugubrious minister played by Rikki Fulton on television?

6   On which channel did Rab C. Nesbitt appear?

7   Name the Scottish comedian and footballer who co-hosted a series of chat shows with Fred Macaulay.

8   Which Scottish presenter fronted *Left Right and Centre*?

9   Name the Scot who moved from *Blue Peter* to *Changing Rooms*.

10 Who presented *Scottish Women*?

11 With which news programme is Jackie Bird associated?

12 What was the name of the character played by Fulton Mackay in *Porridge*?

13 With which kind of television programme is Hazel Irvine associated?

14 What TV role did actor David Tennant take on in 2006?

15 In which Scottish village was the TV series *Hamish MacBeth* filmed?

16 Where was Ronnie Corbett born?

17 Who played the lead role in *Cracker*?

18 Where is the Beechgrove Garden?

19 Who played Private Fraser in *Dad's Army*?

20 Who sang the the theme tune for *Hazell*?

21 What is the real name of the estate known as 'Glenbogle' in the TV series *Monarch of the Glen*?

22 Which character in the second series of *Dr Finlay* was played by Ian Bannen?

23 Who wrote *Tutti Frutti*?

24 Which young Scot moved from the *High Road* to the *Crow Road*?

25 Which actor starred in the 1970s series *Callan* as Lonely?

Answers: p134

General Knowledge 2

1 Who founded Sweetheart Abbey?

2 Where can you see the death mask of Mary, Queen of Scots?

3 What hobby might you pursue at Barns Ness, near Dunbar?

4 Who painted *The Village Politicians* in 1806?

5 A memorial to the writer Gavin Maxwell stands in Monreith Bay near Port William. What form does this memorial take?

6 In which village in Strathclyde are four of the daughters of Robert Burns buried?

7 Name the industrialist and philanthropist who wrote *The Gospel of Wealth*.

8 What television comedy part is Gregor Fisher best known for?

9 Where did John Dewar first set up shop?

10 What is the Kintyre Way?

11 Where is the Merrymass Fair held?

12 Where is the oldest example of a mercat cross still in its original site?

13 Beneath which hills are King Arthur and his knights said to rest?

14 Name the loch by which stands Tibbie Shiel's Inn.

15 Which family of industrialists is associated with the town of Paisley?

16 Where in Lothian was a children's village created by Mrs Stirling Boyd?

17 Which cathedral in Strathclyde claims to be the smallest cathedral in Europe?

18 In which decade did drilling for oil begin in the North Sea?

19 What do the initials SSPCK stand for?

20 Who was the last Scottish king to speak Gaelic?

21 Where were the Churchill Barriers erected during the Second World War?

22 In which region are the Sands of Forvie?

23 To the nearest five miles, how long is the West Highland Way?

24 What do Crieff, Dunblane and Peebles have in common?

25 Who, in the seventeenth century, is said to have predicted the building of the Caledonian Canal?

Answers: p135

Poetry 1

1   Who wrote *The Brus*?
2   Name the Scottish poet who wrote 'The Thrissil and the Rois' while serving as a courtier to James IV.
3   'The King sits in Dunfermline town
    Drinking the blude red wine . . .'
    Which Scottish poem begins with these lines?
4   Which Scottish poet was also a skilled translator and collaborated with his wife on a translation of the works of Franz Kafka?
5   Which Scots poet published a collection of work entitled *Loaves and Fishes*?
6   Which poet and playwright published *True Confessions and New Clichés*?
7   What was the title of the Kilmarnock edition of Robert Burns's poetry?
8   What was the major work of Blind Harry?
9   Which Scottish poet died at Penzance in 1909?
10 Which Gaelic poet received the Queen's Gold Medal for Poetry in 1990?
11 Which eighteenth-century Edinburgh poet wrote 'Auld Reekie'?
12 Who collaborated with Sorley Maclean to produce *Seventeen Poems for Sixpence* in 1940?
13 Which famous noble soldier wrote the following lines?
    'He either fears his fate too much
    Or his deserts are small
    Who dares not put it to the touch
    To win or lose it all.'
14 Who published *A Kist o' Whistles* in 1947?
15 Who was Robert Burns's 'Clarinda'?
16 Who published *Lays of the Scottish Cavaliers* and *Poland, Homer and Other Poems*?
17 Where was Norman MacCaig born?
18 Who wrote *The King's Quair* ?
19 Who wrote the children's poem 'The Land of Counterpane'?
20 Which Scottish poet became Poet Laureate in 2009?
21 Where was James Hogg born?
22 Who wrote 'The Ballad of the D-Day Landings'?
23 Which poet wrote three *Hymns to Lenin*?
24 Which poet published collections entitled *A Man In My Position* and *The Equal Skies*?
25 What was the title of Edwin Morgan's first published collection of poetry?

Answers: p135

Wildlife 1

1. What is the Latin name for the spear thistle, emblem of Scotland?
2. What does the name 'capercaillie' mean?
3. What is the main food of grouse?
4. Which small animal, farmed for over twenty years in Scotland, has escaped into the wild in great numbers over time and now poses a significant threat to many species of wildlife?
5. What is Scotland's largest wild animal?
6. What kind of tree can be seen flourishing particularly well in Rothiemurchus Forest?
7. What kind of bird overwinters on Islay, causing disputes between conservationists and islanders?
8. What is machair?
9. Where do the sika deer in Scotland originate from?
10. Where did the ospreys return to in Scotland?
11. In which decade were reindeer reintroduced to Scotland?
12. Which species of squirrel is larger, the native red or the import from America, the grey?
13. Which two main rivers in Scotland are sources of freshwater mussels that contain pearls?
14. Why is the blue hare so called?
15. Where is the Scottish wildcat most commonly found?
16. What is a Scotch Argus?
17. Which one of Scotland's lochs has the largest number of fish species?
18. Which Scottish nature reserve was the first nature reserve to be established in Britain?
19. What was the first tree to become established in Scotland after the Ice Age?
20. What is the botanical name for Scots Pine?
21. Which animal has recently been reintroduced to Scotland on a trial basis?
22. Where was the last great auk killed?
23. Name the only bird that is unique to Scotland.
24. Where on Scotland's coastline can bottle-nosed dolphins still be seen?
25. Which relative of the weasel was exterminated in Scotland by the end of the nineteenth century?

Answers: p136

Life & Works of Sir Walter Scott

1   Which school in Edinburgh did Sir Walter Scott attend?

2   What ailment struck Scott when he was a young child?

3   When was the *Minstrelsy* first published in a three-volume edition?

4   What were the names of Scott's four brothers?

5   Which literary figure did Scott meet at Adam Ferguson's house when he was 15?

6   What is the name of the female character who faces execution in *Heart of Midlothian*?

7   What is the name of the place where Scott spent much of his early childhood with his parents?

8   How old was Scott when he first went to university?

9   To whom did Scott dedicate the poem 'The Field of Waterloo'?

10 In which century is *Kenilworth* set?

11 Where did Scott move to from Lasswade in 1804?

12 In which year was *Guy Mannering* first published?

13 By which name was Robert Paterson known?

14 Which important event did Scott attend in July 1821?

15 Name the hero of *The Antiquary*.

16 After the visit of George IV to Scotland, what moveable feature of Edinburgh Castle, removed to the Tower of London in 1745, was returned at Scott's request?

17 In which work does the character of John Mowbray feature?

18 When did Scott marry?

19 What was the name of Scott's wife?

20 What is the name of the play by Goethe translated by Scott and published in 1799?

21 What was the title of the work (unpublished) that Scott was working on in his final months?

22 In which novel do Torquil of the Oak and Oliver Proudfute appear?

23 Whom did Scott's son Walter marry?

24 How many (surviving) sons did Scott have?

25 With which two brothers did Scott set up a publishing firm?

Answers: p136

General Knowledge 3

1   Who became head of the House of Stewart after the death of Bonnie Prince Charlie?

2   Name the six former regiments that make up the five regular battalions of the new Royal Regiment of Scotland.

3   Which saint came to Scotland before St Columba and established churches on Iona, Mull and Tiree?

4   When was the first printing press established in Edinburgh?

5   The chief of which clan was given the title *Buichaille nan Eileanan* (Shepherd of the Isles)?

6   Who was the master of Greyfriars Bobby?

7   Who was the first detective in Chicago?

8   Which art gallery in Edinburgh houses the Paolozzi Collection?

9   Where and when was the Revised Book of Common Prayer for Scotland read in public for the first time?

10 What was the name of James VI's scholarly but brutal tutor?

11 Where was the first British Open Golf Championship held?

12 What was the fate of the architect who designed the Scott Monument in Edinburgh?

13 In which trade did the artist Sir Henry Raeburn originally train?

14 What was the name given to the area which included Argyll, Kintyre and nearby islands when Kenneth McAlpin came to the throne?

15 Where was Captain Kidd born?

16 Who led the troops who burnt the Campbell stronghold of Inveraray to the ground in 1644?

17 Who founded the Advocate's Library in Edinburgh?

18 Where is the oldest working mill in Scotland?

19 In which borders village is Tibbie Shiel buried?

20 Where are 'the Twa Brigs'?

21 Where was Scottish racing driver Jim Clark born?

22 Which Scottish city once had the fourth largest cable tram system in the world?

23 In which Scottish city is 'Little France'?

24 What do the letters SQA stand for?

25 Which Lord Provost headed the 'Glasgow's Miles Better' campaign?

Answers: p137

QUESTIONS

1   Where is the Lost Valley?

2   What is the most easterly point on the Scottish mainland?

3   In which city will you find the Howff?

4   What is the largest granite-built church in the British Isles?

5   Where is Stac an Armin?

6   Where will you find Magnus, Clair, Columba, Dunlin and Piper?

7   Where would you go to visit the Clickhimin Broch?

8   What was the name of the Second World War commando training centre near Spean Bridge?

9   Where is the King's Knot?

10 Near which town in Perthshire would you find the Dunfallandy Stone?

11 Where did Edinburgh's Royal Observatory move to in 1896?

12 Where is Argyll's Lodging?

13 What is the Grey Mare's Tail, near Moffat?

14 Where is the site of the sunken Spanish galleon, *Florida*?

15 Where can you see the Loch Faskally Dam?

16 Where is the former home of David Dale?

17 Where is Hugh Miller's Cottage?

18 Where in Peebleshire is said to be the grave of the wizard Merlin?

19 In which city are the McManus Galleries?

20 Where is Inchmahome Priory?

21 Where is the Scottish Rugby Union Museum?

22 In a church in Strathcarron can be seen, scratched on the windows, the names of people evicted from their homes in Glencalvie during the clearances of 1845. What is the name of the church?

23 Where in Scotland are the Open Gold-Panning Championships held annually?

24 In which region of Scotland are the Cairnholy chambered cairns?

25 Where is Black Mount?

Answers: p137

Law & Order

1   What was 'hamesucken'?
2   What is the verdict unique to Scots Law?
3   When was capital punishment abolished in Scotland?
4   What is the name of the supreme court in Scotland for civil matters?
5   When was the first female judge appointed in Scotland?
6   What are the two most commonly reported crimes in Scotland?
7   What is the maximum sentence handed out by the sheriff courts?
8   What is the name for the hearings system which deals with children under the age of sixteen in Scotland?
9   Who was the last person to be hanged in Scotland?
10 What was the name of the young lady who caused a great scandal in Victorian times when she was accused of poisoning her lover with arsenic?
11 What is the name of Edinburgh's prison?
12 What was 'stouthrief'?
13 For what crime was Eugene Chantrelle hanged?
14 Who heads the High Court of Justiciary?
15 What was the most common means of execution of witches in the sixteenth century?
16 Where is Scotland's hospital for the criminally insane?
17 What is the Scottish equivalent of a barrister?
18 Which Scottish university has the largest law school?
19 What is the name of the largest prison in Scotland?
20 What difference between Scots and English Law brought people running across the border to Gretna Green pre-1969?
21 Where is Scotland's first privately run prison?
22 Which Scottish judge was referred to as 'the Jeffreys of Scotland'?
23 Name the eighteenth-century Scottish judge who is remembered for his eccentricity and interest in anthropology as much as for his abilities as a judge.
24 Which Scottish university was the first to appoint a woman as a professor of law?
25 What is the title of the president of the Faculty of Advocates?

Answers: p138

Music 1

1 Which group had a chart hit with 'Don't Leave Me This Way'?
2 What was the instrumental hit of the Average White Band in 1975?
3 Who sang 'Darlin''?
4 In which country did the Bay City Rollers split up?
5 Which band produced an album called 'Street Fighting Years' in 1989?
6 With which kind of music were the Rezillos associated?
7 Where do Del Amitri hail from?
8 Which Scottish rock star was married to Patsy Kensit?
9 Which Glasgow-born artist had a hit in 1956 with 'Rock Island Line'?
10 Who had a hit with the 'Boat That I Row'?
11 Where did the Beatles make their first appearance in Scotland?
12 Which Scottish group produced an album called *The Man Who* . . .?
13 Which Glasgow band brought out a record called 'Now We're Thru' in 1964?
14 Who was the lead singer in the Tourists?
15 On the soundtrack of which film can you hear '(I'm Gonna Be) 500 Miles' by the Proclaimers?
16 Name the Scot who had a hit with 'Personality' in 1974?
17 What was the title of the football song with which Andy Cameron had a hit in 1978?
18 Which street did Gerry Rafferty sing about?
19 Where is the Royal Scottish National Orchestra based?
20 When was the Royal Concert Hall in Glasgow opened?
21 Which band had a hit with 'The Boston Tea Party'?
22 Which band did Midge Ure play in?
23 Who had a hit with 'I Should have Known Better'?
24 What was the name of the lead singer in Marillion?
25 In which year did Pilot have a hit with 'January'?

Answers: p138

Holy People & Holy Places 1

1   Who brought Benedictine monks to Dunfermline?
2   What is the other name by which St Kentigern is known?
3   From which century does Dryburgh Abbey date?
4   Which disciple of St Columba went to Lindisfarne to convert Northumbria?
5   Where is John Knox buried?
6   When is St Andrew's Day?
7   Who became minister of St Giles in Edinburgh in 1560?
8   Which football club is named after a saint?
9   In which part of Scotland did St Regulus carry out his mission?
10 Where is the Apprentice Pillar?
11 Where is St Mungo's Chapel?
12 In which cathedral were James V and Mary of Guise married?
13 Where is Scotland's Buddhist Monastery and Tibetan Centre?
14 Who founded the Free Church in Scotland?
15 Which Scottish king founded Holyrood, Kelso and Jedburgh Abbeys among others?
16 Orkney has an annual festival in honour of which saint?
17 Which order of monks lived at Deer Abbey?
18 Who was responsible for the founding of the first university in Scotland?
19 On which island are ancient kings of Scotland and Norway buried?
20 With which part of Scotland is St Cuthbert associated?
21 What is the name of the Catholic martyr who became Scotland's first post-Reformation saint?
22 Which cathedral in Scotland survived the Reformation relatively unscathed?
23 From which century do the ruins of Elgin Cathedral date?
24 In which abbey is James III buried?
25 Where did St Baldred live?

Answers: p139

General Knowledge 4

1   Which university medical school became the first to admit a woman in 1869?

2   Which Scottish poet wrote a Scots translation of *Cyrano de Bergerac*?

3   Who became Secretary of the newly formed Scottish Miners' Federation in 1886?

4   When was the hydro-electric power station opened at Ben Cruachan?
    a) 1965 b) 1948 c) 1971

5   Put the following rivers in order of length, starting with the longest: Tweed, Spey, Clyde, Tay.

6   What are the defining qualities of Harris tweed?

7   Which political party was inaugurated at Stirling in 1928?

8   When was the Highlands and Islands Development Board created?
    a) 1956 b) 1959 c) 1969

9   Where can you take a trip on the SS *Sir Walter Scott*?

10 What was the fiery cross used for?

11 When did the wearing of tartan clothing become illegal in Scotland?

12 What was the name of the ship in which Bonnie Prince Charlie sailed from France to Scotland?

13 What did Margaret Chalmers, Maria Riddell, Elizabeth Paton, Jenny Clow, Anna Park, Agnes Maclehose, Jean Armour and Mary Campbell have in common?

14 When was the Anatomy Act passed, giving teachers of anatomy access to a legal supply of bodies for dissection? a) 1747 b) 1838 c) 1832

15 Which Scottish island was once owned by Keith Schellenberg?

16 In what year was Glasgow's University of Strathclyde established?

17 Which Scottish actor became the tenth Dr Who in 2006?

18 What is Scotland's rarest mammal?

19 Where is the Strait of Corryvreckan?

20 During which king's reign was the religious centre of Scotland moved from Iona to Dunkeld?

21 In which year did William Wallace become an outlaw?

22 What sport is played by Kyles Athletic?

23 What is the name of the female character whose life story is told in *A Scots Quair*?

24 Which three Williams' names are associated with the history of publishing in Scotland?

25 Which famous Scottish socialist politician and activist died in 1923?

Answers: p139

History 1

1 In which year was the Declaration of Arbroath made?

2 When was the Stone of Destiny stolen from Westminster Abbey?

3 Where did Bonnie Prince Charlie raise his standard in 1745, to rally the support of the Highland chiefs?

4 In which year was Mary, Queen of Scots, forced to abdicate the throne of Scotland?

5 Which entire Roman legion was lost in an attempt to subdue the rebellious Scots?

6 In the reign of which king did the 'Bloody Assizes' take place?

7 In which year did Bonnie Prince Charlie die?

8 In which year did James II lay seige to Roxburgh Castle?

9 Upon whose death did Malcolm Canmore succeed to the throne?

10 Who succeeded Malcolm II to the throne?

11 Who killed Duncan I?

12 In which year was John Balliol forced to surrender his crown to Edward I?

13 Where was Charles I held prisoner prior to his trial at Westminster?

14 Who became the only Scottish royal saint more than two centuries after her death?

15 Where was Mary, Queen of Scots, held prisoner in the period leading up to her trial and execution?

16 Against whose forces were the Covenanters successful in the Battle of Drumclog?

17 In which year did the Battle of Solway Moss take place?

18 In which century did Orkney come under Scottish rule?

19 In which year was the Treaty of Northampton signed?

20 Whose forces defeated the army of Edward I at Stirling Bridge?

21 In which year did the first expedition to Darien set out?

22 What was the name of the great warship built as pride of the navy of James IV?

23 What was the name of the man who captured William Wallace and took him to London where he was executed?

24 Whom did Andrew Melville refer to as 'God's sillie vassal'?

25 How many Scottish representatives were allowed to sit in parliament at Westminster while Cromwell was in power?

Answers: p140

Travel

1. In what year did the Tay Bridge Disaster take place?
2. Off which main road is 'the Lang Whang' a part?
3. Which company runs most of the ferry services from the mainland to the Western Isles?
4. How long did it take to build the Caledonian Canal?
   a) 5 years b) 18 years c) 15 years
5. What is the name of the canal that was built between 1818 and 1828 to link Edinburgh with the Forth and Clyde Canal at Falkirk?
6. What was the name of the station at the west end of Edinburgh's city centre, beside the Caledonian Hotel, which closed in 1965?
7. How many locks are there on the Caledonian Canal?
8. What was the name of the waterway opened in 1790 to forge a link for shipping between the Atlantic and the North Sea?
9. In which year was the Forth Rail Bridge opened?
10. What is the name of the £120 million road bridge across the upper Firth of Forth opened in 2008?
11. What kind of bridge is the Erskine Bridge?
12. When were Glasgow and Edinburgh linked by railway?
13. What is the nearest railway station to St Andrews in Fife?
14. How would you travel to Knoydart Peninsula?
15. Where is Sumburgh Airport?
16. When and where did the last tram run in Scotland?
17. Which road in Scotland is most frequently blocked by snow in winter?
18. Where does the Crinan Canal run?
19. Which road crosses the border into England at Gretna Green?
20. In which part of Scotland is Electric Brae?
21. Where was the hairpin bend known as 'the Devil's Elbow' (now replaced by a safer, straighter road)?
22. From where can you take a ferry across the River Almond to the Rosebery Estate on the banks of the Forth?
23. Before the Forth Road Bridge was built, what was the most easterly road bridge across the Forth?
24. Where is the northerly terminus of the A9?
25. In which decade was Glasgow Central railway station opened?

Answers: p140

Myth & Mystery, Magic & Superstition 1

1   Which tree is believed to protect against evil spirits?
2   What is the name of the monster of Loch Morar?
3   What is a kelpie?
4   What is the name of the hill near Inverness where fiddlers played at a fairy ball?
5   Who prophesied the fall of the Mackenzies of Seaforth?
6   What should be placed in the hand of a newborn child?
7   What was the name of the black magician, calling himself 'the wickedest man on earth', who had a house on the shores of Loch Ness?
8   What was the purpose of a lykewake?
9   Where is the lighthouse whose keepers mysteriously disappeared?
10 What was the name of the seer who is said to have foretold the death of Alexander III?
11 Why should the shells of boiled eggs be turned upside down and smashed once empty?
12 Who is Domhnull Dubh?
13 Where is the community where scientists were baffled by the ability of the people to grow marvellous crops in barren and inhospitable conditions?
14 Which Scottish leader was reputed to have been in league with the Devil and to have been killed by a silver bullet when he fell in battle?
15 What powers did the waters of the Fiddler's Well in Cromarty supposedly have?
16 Which prominent Scot of the seventeenth century was said to have beaten the Devil in a card game, which led to the Devil throwing a table into a pond?
17 To which holy man did a water monster, now thought to be Nessie, appear on Loch Ness in the sixth century AD?
18 What is the unusual ghost that is said to haunt Drumlanrig Castle?
19 Which playing card is known as 'the Curse of Scotland'?
20 What is the colour of the spiritual creature known as a glastaig?
21 What was the name of the female seer from Perthshire who is supposed to have predicted the Clearances and the Tay Bridge disaster?
22 What powers could a selkie have?
23 What are the magical powers of the fairy flag in Dunvegan Castle?
24 On which island do the ghostly shapes of Viking invaders appear from time to time?
25 What are brunaidh?

Answers: p141

General Knowledge 5

1   Which Scottish poet, songwriter and eccentric, who died in 2006, was responsible for *Life in a Scotch Sitting Room, Volume 2*?
2   Which Scottish news programme did Mary Marquis present?
3   Who was the founder and director of the Celtic Film Festival?
4   Which film star did a voice-over for an SNP party political broadcast in 1991?
5   When was the Edinburgh Festival launched?
6   When was the village of Forteviot rebuilt?
    a) the 1690s b) the 1920s c) the 1860sc
7   In which year did entertainer Jimmy Logan die?
8   What was the fictional name for the setting of the television series *Hamish MacBeth*?
9   Which powerful position was George Robertson appointed to in 1999?
10 Which city has a Camera Obscura?
11 In which country did the trial take place of the Lockerbie Bombing suspects?
12 What were the titles of the three books in *A Scots Quair*?
13 Where are the headquarters of BBC Radio Scotland?
14 Which Scottish businessman bought the controlling share in Rangers Football Club in 1988?
15 With which political party is the name of Donald Gorrie associated?
16 In which decade was the Special Unit set up in Barlinnie Prison?
17 Where was the poet William Soutar born?
18 Who was lead singer of the Communards?
19 When was 'the Rough Wooing'?
20 Which Scots-born sailor fought against the British on the ship *Bonhomme Richard*?
21 When was the Poll Tax introduced in Scotland?
22 Who printed the first *Encyclopaedia Britannica*?
23 Which Scottish field marshall founded the British Legion?
24 What is the name for the Scottish school founded and run on the principles of Kurt Hahn?
25 Which Scottish author spent much of his childhood at Sandyknowe in the Borders?

28

Literature 1

1. What is the name of the Clyde puffer in *Para Handy*?
2. Who wrote *Whisky Galore*?
3. Which nineteenth-century Scottish churchman and writer founded *The Bookman* and *Woman at Home* and was editor of *The British Weekly*?
4. What is the name of the famous fictional character created by Sir Arthur Conan Doyle?
5. Which Scots writer wrote *The French Revolution: A History*?
6. Which Scottish novelist lived at Abbotsford?
7. Which modern Scottish novelist won the 1993 Booker Prize?
8. What was the title of the book that won the Booker Prize in 1993?
9. What are the names of the three autobiographical books written by Eric Linklater?
10. Who wrote *The Blue Fairy Book*?
11. What is the title of Cliff Hanley's autobiographical account of life in Glasgow?
12. Under which name did Sir Walter Scott originally publish his novels?
13. Name the contemporary novelist who wrote *The Crow Road* and *The Wasp Factory*.
14. Which nineteenth-century Scottish writer wrote *The House with the Green Shutters*?
15. Name the book written by Irvine Welsh that was made into a box-office success at the cinema.
16. Who wrote *Lanark*?
17. *A Treatise on Human Nature* was one of the most important pieces of philosophical writing in the eighteenth century. Who wrote it?
18. In which century did the Scots historian Thomas Carlyle live?
19. Name the author of *Cloud Cuckoo Land* and *Black Sparta*.
20. What was the famous trilogy of novels written by Lewis Grassic Gibbon?
21. Who wrote *The Thirty-Nine Steps*?
22. Inspector Rebus is the central character in several books by which crime writer?
23. Who wrote *The Trick Is To Keep Breathing*?
24. What was the name of the first book published by Robin Jenkins?
25. What was the name given to a school of Scottish fiction in the nineteenth century characterized by romanticism and sentimentality?

Answers: p142

QUESTIONS

Life & Works of John Buchan

1 What was the occupation of John Buchan's father?
2 What was the name of his younger sister who died when she was a young child?
3 From where did the family move to Glasgow?
4 What serious injury did John Buchan suffer as a child?
5 What school did John Buchan attend in Glasgow?
6 To whom did John Buchan dedicate *Scholar Gipsies*?
7 In which publication was *John Burnet of Barnes* serialized before being published as a novel?
8 Under whom did John Buchan take up his first post abroad?
9 In which magazine was *The Power House* serialized?
10 Which novel was originally given the title *The Black Stone*?
11 The *Nelson History of the War* was published in how many parts?
12 In which novel did Dickson McCunn first appear?
13 In which year did John Buchan accept the post of Governor-General of Canada?
14 In which two books do we encounter Richard Hannay?
15 What is the name of Buchan's autobiography, published in 1941?
16 How many children did John Buchan and his wife have?
17 In which book does the character of John Laputa feature?
18 What is the title of the last novel written by John Buchan?
19 Who made the first film of *The Thirty-Nine Steps*?
20 What is the title of the poem for which Buchan won the Newdigate Prize for Poetry?
21 What was John Buchan's chosen title as a peer?
22 What was the name of Buchan's first novel, published in 1895?
23 In which year did Buchan join the Intelligence Corps?
24 What was the name of Buchan's wife?
25 In which year was John Buchan first elected to parliament?

Answers: p142

Aberdeen

1 Aberdeen once had an opera house, which then became the Tivoli Theatre. What was its name?

2 Where is the statue of Prince Albert?

3 In which year did the last hanging take place at Craiginches Prison?

4 Name the architect who designed the façade of St Nicholas's Church in Union Street?

5 Aberdeen is known as 'the Granite City'. What is the name of the great hole in the ground from which granite was once quarried?

6 Name the three hills upon which Aberdeen was built.

7 When was Marischal College founded?

8 Who founded King's College?

9 In which year in the 1980s did Aberdeen Football Club win the European Cup-Winners Cup?

10 Which poet is commemorated with a statue outside the Grammar School?

11 What is the name of Aberdeen's cathedral?

12 Which flower was depicted on the coat of arms of Old Aberdeen?

13 In which century was the Town House built?

14 Which newspaper was founded in 1748?

15 Which museum is housed at St Luke's House?

16 Where does the Mercat Cross now stand?

17 What is the city's railway station called?

18 Which queen moved from St Nicholas Street to Queen's Cross?

19 What is the motto of Aberdeen?

20 Which historian wrote *The Silver City by the Grey North Sea*?

21 Where is the statue in memory of the men who lost their lives in the Piper Alpha disaster?

22 Who wrote *A Thousand Years of Aberdeen*?

23 Which theatre in Aberdeen was opened in 1906?

24 Which student residence in Aberdeen was the first to accommodate students of both sexes?

25 What is the oldest street in the city?

Answers: p143

General Knowledge 6

QUESTIONS

1 Where is McCaig's Folly?
2 What are the names of the three lochs in the Caledonian Canal?
3 Where is the largest model railway in Britain?
4 When did David Dale begin work on his project at New Lanark?
5 Who was the wife of John Balliol?
6 Where is the Logan Botanic Garden?
7 Where is the National Trust for Scotland's Tenement House?
8 What is the name of the highest village in Scotland?
9 Who played the part of Janet in *Dr Finlay's Casebook*?
10 In which city was footballer Graeme Souness born?
11 When was the Bank of Scotland founded?
   a) the 1570s b) the 1690s c) the 1820s
12 Which Scot discovered the Victoria Falls?
13 Which Scottish town was crowned 'Scotland's most dismal' in the Carbuncle Awards of 2001 and 2005?
14 Which Scots actress was 'Supergran'?
15 Which historic event took place on July 1, 1999?
16 Who was captain of the 1974 Scottish World Cup Squad?
17 Where is the Fife Folk Museum?
18 Which Scottish explorer discovered the source of the Blue Nile?
19 Who painted the portrait of Robert Burns which hangs in the Scottish National Portrait Gallery?
20 Which future king of Scotland married Anne Hyde when he was Duke of York?
21 The daughters of which sixteenth-century earl were known as the Seven Pearls of Loch Leven?
22 Where, near Edinburgh, can you view the wonders of the deep all around you from a transparent tunnel?
23 Where is John Duns Scotus said to have been born?
24 What was the profession of Sir William Burrell?
25 What strange occurrence was reported in *The Inverness Courier* in 1933?

Answers: p143

32

Feasts, Festivals & Fun

1 Where in Fife is the Links Market held every year?
2 In which month are 'the Honest Toun' celebrations held?
3 What is set alight during the Shetland festival of Up-Helly-Aa?
4 What is the name of the fair held annually in St Andrews?
5 In which month does the Edinburgh Festival begin every year?
6 What is celebrated on 25 January?
7 When do you 'dook for apples'?
8 Which town hosts the Great Glen Sheepdog Trials each year?
9 In which month is the Braemar Highland Gathering held each year?
10 In which town is the Beltane Festival held?
11 In which area of Scotland are the Common Ridings held?
12 Which university stages the annual Kate Kennedy procession?
13 On which day of the year is the Burning of the Clavie ceremony held?
14 Which date is still sometimes called 'Gowkie Day'?
15 When is Handsel Monday?
16 In which Scottish town is Whuppity Scoorie celebrated?
17 In which city do the World Pipe Band Championships take place each summer?
18 Which saint is remembered on June 9?
19 How do the energetic celebrate 1 May in Edinburgh?
20 When is St Andrew's Day?
21 What was Shrove Tuesday once known as in Scotland?
22 Which festival is Britain's second largest arts festival?
23 Where does the Boys Ploughing Match take place annually?
24 Which town in Fife has a New Year torch procession?
25 Where would you see 'the Burry Man'?

Answers: p144

Tunes That Made Them Famous

1   With which two famous characters in history is the song 'Over the Sea to Skye' associated?

2   Who first hit the British Top Ten with 'Shout'?

3   Which folk-singing duo made 'Flower of Scotland' popular?

4   Which pop group sang 'Shang-a-Lang'?

5   Who wrote 'Ae Fond Kiss'?

6   Who is remembered for 'Roamin' in the Gloamin'?

7   Who wrote 'Charlie is my Darling'?

8   Which Scottish entertainer asked Donald where his troosers were?

9   Which Scots lass hit the big time with '9 to 5'?

10   Who wrote 'Jerusalem the Golden'?

11   Who wrote 'Afton Water'?

12   Who had a chart hit with 'Baker Street'?

13   Who sang about his old man, the dustman?

14   Which battle is remembered by 'Hey, Johnny Cope'?

15   Which Scottish singing duo sang about 'Sunshine on Leith'?

16   Who composed 'The Bonnie Wells o' Wearie'?

17   Which items of footwear did Billy Connolly praise in song?

18   Name the band which asks 'Why Does It Always Rain on Me?'

19   Who wrote 'O, My Luve's Like a Red, Red Rose'?

20   Which young Scots lass sang 'Ma, He's Making Eyes at Me'?

21   What was the song that made Will Fyffe famous?

22   With which song did Lulu win the Eurovision Song Contest?

23   Who is remembered for 'The Bluebell Polka'?

24   About whom was the lament 'Will Ye No' Come Back Again?' written?

25   Who wrote 'Scots Wha Hae'?

Answers: p144

Great Scots 1

1 What was the name of the Scottish educationist who founded Summerhill School?

2 Where did Mary Slessor work as a missionary?

3 In which country did Samuel Greig achieve fame?

4 In which century was John Duns Scotus born?

5 Who wrote *Sketchbook of Popular Geology*?

6 In honour of whom were the villages of North Queensferry and South Queensferry named?

7 Which philosopher wrote a many-volumed history of England between 1754 and 1762?

8 Which great Scot was sentenced to the galleys in 1547?

9 Name the famous Scottish artist who started his career by painting miniatures.

10 Who died in the Palazzo Muti in Rome in 1788?

11 Which famous Scot was married to John George Stewart-Murray, Marquess of Tullibardine, in 1899?

12 Of which university did Adam Smith become Lord Rector in 1787?

13 What was the name of Flora Macdonald's husband?

14 Which Scots writer published a collection of translations of the work of several writers entitled *Rites of Passage*?

15 Who was stabbed to death by Robert the Bruce?

16 Which Scottish writer was Governor-General of Canada in the 1930s?

17 Which great Scottish inventor founded the journal *Science*?

18 Who wrote a twenty-volume history of Scotland entitled *Rerum Scoticarum Historia*?

19 Which king introduced the Order of the Knights Templar to Scotland?

20 Who established the second law of thermodynamics?

21 What was the title held by James Burnett, judge and anthropologist of the eighteenth century?

22 Which well-known Scottish writer published a biography of Mungo Park?

23 What was the Christian name of the 1st Earl Haig of Bemersyde?

24 Who was the geologist who published *A Theory of the Earth* in the eighteenth century?

25 Which early twentieth-century Scots political activist campaigned for a Scottish Workers' Republic?

Answers: p145

General Knowledge 7

1   Name the village that is home to Skibo Castle, made famous by Madonna and Guy Ritchie's wedding there in 2000.

2   What was the name of the Kirkcudbright fishing boat that sank off the Isle of Man in January 2000?

3   What is the name of the man who composed the fanfare for the opening of the Scottish Parliament?

4   What is the name of the woman who has become known as 'the Cashmere Queen'?

5   What kind of dog is the black dog which features on Black and White Whisky bottles?

6   By which name are the islands sometimes called ' the Seven Hunters' more commonly known?

7   From whom did Edinburgh Council buy Calton Hill in 1725?

8   What was the approximate final cost of the Scottish Parliament Building?

9   What was moved from Calton Hill to Blackford Hill in Edinburgh in 1896?

10 How old was James IV when he took part in the Battle of Sauchieburn?

11 When was the last woman executed for witchcraft in Scotland?
    a) 1678 b) 1727 c) 1809

12 In which century did the crime of witchcraft first appear in the statute book in Scotland?

13 What is sung as Scotland's national anthem before rugby internationals?

14 Name the Scottish singer who rose to fame after taking part in *The Big Time* in 1980.

15 Which Scottish writer was inspired to write his best-loved book by childhood visits to Moat Brae House in Dumfries?

16 Whom did politician Gordon Brown marry in 2000?

17 What are the two towns at each end of the West Highland Way?

18 Which TV personality published *Scotland: Story of a Nation*?

19 In which year was Alex Salmond born?

20 What is the name of the Scottish island that was used for the BBC Television programme *Castaway* in 2000?

21 Which Scottish mountain has a power station inside it?

22 Where in Scotland is the Queen's Gallery, built to house works of art from the Queen's Royal Collection?

23 What was the last lighthouse in Scotland to be automated?

24 With which health scare was John Barr's shop in Wishaw associated?

25 Which MSP and stalwart of the Scottish National Party died, aged 60, in March 2006?

Answers: p145

Scotland & the Media

1 Who became editor-in-chief of Scotsman Publications Ltd in 1986?

2 Name the company which publishes *The Sunday Post*.

3 By which name was *The Herald* previously known?

4 The paper which was once called *The North British Daily Mail* is now known as what?

5 In which decade did the *Scottish Daily News* make a brief appearance?

6 What is the name of Magnus Magnusson's TV presenter daughter?

7 What is the name of Scotland's oldest-surviving journal?

8 Which Scottish daily newspaper moved its offices to a new site in the year 2000?

9 In which century was the *Scots Magazine* first published?

10 Name the Scot who was director-general of the BBC from 1927 to 1938.

11 Of which paper was Alastair Dunnett editor before he became editor of *The Scotsman*?

12 Which newspaper did John Gordon edit from 1928 to 1952?

13 With which Scottish newspaper is Oor Wullie associated?

14 In which century was the *Edinburgh Evening Courant* first published?

15 What is the English name for *Comadaidh Craolaidh Gàidhlig*?

16 What was the name of the company formed by John Logie Baird in 1925?

17 In which decade was Scotland first enabled to receive television broadcasts?

18 Which company owns the Aberdeen *Evening Express*?

19 With which city is the *Evening Times* associated?

20 With which city is the *Press and Journal* associated?

21 What was the name of the television programme presented by Kirsty Wark on BBC Four (2009)?

22 Which group owns *The Scotsman*?

23 Which female TV presenter was chosen to front the Channel 4 programme *Dotcomedy*?

24 Suzie McGuire made her name as a presenter with which radio station?

25 When was Grampian Television first launched?

Answers: p146

Rugby

1   Which former Scottish rugby international player was known as 'the White Shark'?

2   The first Rugby World Cup Sevens took place in Scotland. In which year?

3   How many times did Scotland win the Grand Slam between 1925 and 1990?

4   Who was captain of the Scottish rugby team when Scotland won the Grand Slam in 1990?

5   In what year did the first rugby international take place between England and Scotland?

6   When was the first Calcutta Cup match?

7   When was Murrayfield Stadium first opened by the SRU?

8   Which member of the royal family is the patron of Scottish Rugby?

9   Who were 'the Three Bears'?

10   In 1997 one rugby club won the League Championship, the Tennents Cup, the Border League and the Melrose Sevens Tournament. Which club?

11   How many players were in each team for the first-ever rugby international?

12   Which team won the Scottish Championship for the first five seasons between 1974 and 1978?

13   When did Gavin Hastings retire as captain of the Scottish team?

14   What was the name of the captain of the Scottish team for the first Scottish Grand Slam victory?

15   Where were international matches played in Scotland between 1899 and 1925?

16   What record did Scott Hastings achieve during his years as a Scottish international player?

17   Which club plays at the Greenyards?

18   In which year was the first ever seven-a-side tournament held in Melrose?

19   Who is Scotland's most capped rugby player?

20   How many times did Scotland win the Triple Crown between 1883 and 1998?

21   What part does a grouse play in Scottish Rugby?

22   How many divisions are there in the BT Scotland Premiership?

23   How many times was Scott Hastings capped for Scotland?

24   What illness prevented commentator Bill McLaren from pursuing his career as a player?

25   In which Olympic Games will rugby sevens be admitted to the Olympic movement?

Answers: p146

Politics 1

1   Who became presiding officer of the Scottish Parliament after it was opened in 1999?

2   Where will you find a Gaelic Bible in the House of Commons?

3   In which year did Alex Salmond return as leader of the SNP?

4   Who was the leader of the Scottish Conservative Party at the time of the Conservative Party Conference in September 2000?

5   Which Euro MP was dubbed 'Madame Ecosse'?

6   Who was education minister at the time of the furore over the SQA exam results confusion in 2000?

7   How many Scottish representatives sat in Westminster after the Scottish Reform Bill of 1832?

8   What were the names of the two men who founded the Scottish Labour Party in 1888?

9   In which year were the headquarters of the secretary of state for Scotland moved from Westminster to St Andrew's House?

10   In which year in the twentieth century was a Scottish Covenant drawn up, calling for a Scottishc Parliament within the UK?

11   In March 1979, what percentage of the whole Scottish electorate voted in favour of a Scottish assembly? (Answer to the nearest per cent)

12   What position did Donald Dewar hold in the new Scottish Parliament?

13   Who was voted national chairman of the Young Communist League in 1952?

14   During which years was Arthur Balfour prime minister of Great Britain?

15   Name the Scottish peer who was prime minister from 1963 to 1964.

16   Who replaced Sir Alec Douglas-Home as leader of the Conservative Party?

17   Who was elected as leader of the SNP following the resignation of Alex Salmond in 2000?

18   Who was chief executive of the SNP from 1994 to 1999?

19   Where is former Labour leader John Smith buried?

20   What cabinet position was Sarah Boyack appointed to in the new Scottish Parliament of 1999?

21   Who became prime minister on the resignation of Lord Derby, in 1852?

22   Which nationalist thinker published *Account of a Conversation concerning a Right Regulation of Governments for the Common Good of Mankind* anonymously in 1704?

23   Who led a work-in at Upper Clyde Shipbuilders in 1971?

24   Which former leader of Red Clydeside died in 1923?

25   Who were the two contenders for leadership of the Labour Party in Scotland after the death of Donald Dewar?

Answers: p147

General Knowledge 8

1   Who retired as Bishop of Edinburgh in 2000?

2   What is the name of the children's entertainment group composed of Nicky, Spatz and Mr P?

3   Which legal ghost is said to haunt Edinburgh's Greyfriars Kirkyard?

4   Put the following towns in order north to south: Kingussie, Aviemore, Pitlochry?

5   Bill Millin became known as 'the Mad Piper' during the Second World War. Why?

6   Which eminent Scottish doctor was obstetrician to Queen Charlotte Sophia?

7   Where in Fife is Fife Animal Park?

8   Which mountain by Loch Broom was sold in 2000?

9   What is 'the great chieftain o' the puddin' race'?

10   Which football team did Frank McAvennie play for?

11   The flight between which two Scottish islands achieved recognition as the shortest scheduled flight in the world?

12   Where did the Great Scottish Swim 2009 take place?

13   Where are the ruins of Rob Roy's house?

14   Numbers of snow buntings and ptarmigans have decreased sharply in Scotland in recent years. What is believed to be the reason for this?

15   Which castle is the largest in Scotland?

16   When was the nuclear processing plant at Dounreay built?

17   Which TV series was inspired by the work of Ian Stephen, Peterhead-born psychologist?

18   What is the name of the architect of the new Scottish Parliament Building who died in July 2000?

19   Which city hosts the Scottish Storytelling Festival?

20   Which bird, extinct after the late nineteenth century in Scotland, has been reintroduced to the country since the 1990s?

21   Which Scottish island was declared unsafe by the Ministry of Defence between 1945 and 1990?

22   Which leader of the Labour Party is buried on Iona?

23   With which famous Scottish musician does accordionist Phil Cunningham perform and record?

24   Which former member of Runrig has become a politician?

25   Name the engineer responsible for the construction of the Forth Railway Bridge.

Answers: p147

Architecture

1   Which architect designed the Glasgow School of Art?

2   Who designed the Observatory on Edinburgh's Calton Hill in 1818?

3   Who designed the Edinburgh Academy Building?

4   Where is the Winter Gardens Pavilion designed by Alex Stephen?

5   Who submitted the winning design for the Burrell Gallery in Glasgow?

6   Who designed the National Wallace Monument in Stirling?

7   What is a 'black house'?

8   For whom did Charles Rennie Mackintosh design Hill House in Helensburgh?

9   What is a 'broch'?

10 Who designed Fettes College, the Bank of Scotland headquarters on the Mound and the Royal Infirmary in Edinburgh?

11 What were the names of William Adam's two most famous architect sons?

12 Which Scottish architect designed Coventry Cathedral?

13 Which young architect was responsible for the design of Edinburgh's New Town?

14 What is the name of the school close to the west end of the city of Edinburgh designed by William Henry Playfair?

15 What was the name of the architect who designed the famous Templeton's Carpet Factory in Glasgow?

16 What was the name of the school in Glasgow, now a museum of education, designed by Charles Rennie Mackintosh?

17 What is a 'but and ben'?

18 What was the name of the architect who designed the original building of Hopetoun House?

19 Who designed the Scottish National War Memorial?

20 Which castle in Ayrshire is regarded as one of Robert Adam's finest achievements?

21 What is the name of the only church designed by Charles Rennie Mackintosh?

22 Which Scottish architect designed Blackfriars Bridge in London?

23 Who designed Moray Place in Edinburgh?

24 What was the name of the architect who designed the Royal High School building on Edinburgh's Regent Road?

25 Who designed the Chatelherault Hunting Lodge?

Answers: p148

Dundee

1. Which theatre company is based in Tay Square?
2. Which famous missionary's life is commemorated in stained glass in the McManus Galleries?
3. Who designed the Morgan Tower?
4. What is the name of the city's largest park?
5. In which street did William McGonagall live?
6. What was 'the Fifie'?
7. When did Dundee become a royal burgh?
8. Who designed the first Tay Bridge?
9. Whose statue stands in front of the McManus Galleries?
10. What was the name of the whaling vessel from Dundee which was used by Sir Ernest Shackleton in his polar voyage?
11. What is the name of the oldest British warship afloat, which is anchored in the city's docks?
12. What is the name of Dundee's observatory?
13. In which month does the Dundee City Festival take place?
14. Which famous women's long-distance runner was born in Dundee?
15. Which famous rock band of the 1970s came from Dundee?
16. Which king granted Dundee its royal charter?
17. What is the nickname for Dundee United?
18. When was the University of Dundee founded?
19. Which character in horror fiction was created in Dundee?
20. When was Dundee stormed and plundered by the forces of General Monck?
21. In which decade was the Dundee and Newtyle Railway opened?
22. Which family owned the Dens Mills?
23. Which family owned the Camperdown Works?
24. What is the proper name of 'the Coffin Mill'?
25. Who was provost of Dundee from 1788 to 1819?

Answers: p148

Bonnie Prince Charlie

1 What was the exact date of Prince Charles Edward Stewart's birth?
2 In which year was Charles's brother Henry born?
3 In which year did his mother die?
4 Charles went on tour in the year 1737. To which part of Europe did his travels take him?
5 In which year did Charles see his father for the last time?
6 Who led the French fleet into the Channel in the attempt to invade England in 1744?
7 Who were 'the Seven Men of Glenmoriston'?
8 Where was Flora Macdonald taken to for imprisonment after her arrest?
9 Who led the troops against the Jacobite forces at the Battle of Falkirk?
10 What was the name of the Englishman among 'the Seven Men of Moidart'?
11 What was the first battle victory for the Jacobite cause?
12 Which part of Edinburgh remained in the possession of the government troops after Charles's entry to Edinburgh?
13 In which month was Carlisle captured?
14 In which month was the decision taken to retreat from England?
15 After which event in the '45 did Charles lose the support of Lord George Murray for a while?
16 In which year did Charles meet Clementina Walkinshaw?
17 Where had the Jacobite forces reached when the decision was made to turn back?
18 How many months did Charles remain in Scotland after Culloden?
19 When Charles revisited London in 1750, how long did he stay?
20 In which year was Charles's daughter born?
21 In which year did Charles convert to the Protestant faith?
22 Who was the last man to be executed for his part in the '45 rebellion?
23 In which year did Clementina Walkinshaw leave Charles?
24 Whom did Charles marry in 1772?
25 What was the name of the man for whom Charles's wife left him in 1780?

QUESTIONS

Answers: p149

General Knowledge 9

1   In which year did the Ibrox Stadium disaster take place?
2   At which Scottish prison did riots take place in 1979?
3   In which city was Jim Watt, the boxer, born?
4   Name the former newspaper editor who became a leading light in Scotland's oil industry.
5   Which publisher became Queen's Printer for Scotland in 1862?
6   What activity is associated with the letters RSCDS? What do the letters stand for?
7   Name the Scot who discovered penicillin.
8   What profession was followed by Robert Louis Stevenson's famous grandfather?
9   Which engineer was responsible for the building of the Menai Suspension Bridge?
10 In which century did Thomas the Rhymer live?
11 In which industry did the Thomson family of Dundee make their fortune before branching out into the newspaper industry?
12 Who introduced 'the Maiden' to Scotland in the sixteenth century?
13 When did the *Comet* make her first trip?
14 What does SCWS stand for?
15 What kind of plant are the gardens of Achamore House on Gigha famed for?
16 What is the former Advocate's Library in Edinburgh now known as?
17 Who founded St Andrew's University?
18 Who invented the adhesive postage stamp?
19 Who wrote *A Letter of Adieu to the Scotch*?
20 Where was the National Covenant of 1683 subscribed?
21 In which decade was a public postal system installed in Scotland?
22 Which university in Scotland was the first to have a chair in medicine?
23 Which port was merged with the city of Edinburgh in 1920?
24 What does 'sonsie' mean??
25 How many education authorities are there in Scotland?

Answers: p149

Golf

1   Name the Scottish woman golfer who won the Women's British Open in 2009.
2   Which Scottish golfer won the British Open with a set of clubs which he had made himself?
3   In which year was the British Open held for the last time at Musselburgh?
4   Where was Old Tom Morris born?
5   Where was the first 18-hole golf course made in Scotland?
6   Which west coast golf course is renowned for its opening hole?
7   What is the name of the championship course at Gullane?
8   In which year did the first British Open take place?
9   What is the name of the first golf club to be founded in Scotland?
10 Which Scottish king banned the playing of golf?
11 Which self-proclaimed Scot won the British Open in 1985?
12 Where is the Scottish Golf Union based?
13 Who won the first British Open?
14 In which year did Tom Watson win the British Open at Turnberry?
15 Which is the Road Hole on the Old Course at St Andrews?
16 Where is 'home' to the Honourable Company of Edinburgh Golfers?
17 Which Scottish golfer has earned a reputation as 'the best player never to win a Major'?
18 How many Scottish courses have hosted the British Open since it began?
19 Which course hosts the Scottish Open on the European Tour?
20 Which Scot won the championship belt of the British Open for the third time in a row in 1870?
21 Who scored the first hole-in-one recorded in the British Open?
22 In which year did Sandy Lyle become the first Briton to win the US Masters?
23 When did Carnoustie first host the British Open?
24 What is the name of the main course at Gleneagles?
25 How many holes were there at St Andrews before it was made into an 18-hole course in 1764?

Answers: p150

Films & Film Stars 1

1 With which actress did Scottish actor Tom Conti star in *Heavenly Pursuits*?

2 Name the Scots star of *Sliding Doors*.

3 Which Scottish actor played the male romantic lead in *Moulin Rouge*?

4 Who played the object of Gregory's desire in *Gregory's Girl*?

5 Who directed *Shallow Grave*?

6 Where was *Venus Peter* filmed?

7 Which film, based on a book by Alastair Maclean, was filmed on the island of Mull?

8 In which Bill Forsyth film did actor Bill Paterson find himself caught up in ice-cream wars?

9 Where was *Ring of Bright Water* filmed?

10 Which bridge features in the film of *The Thirty-Nine Steps*?

11 Where is the setting for *Small Faces*?

12 Who directed *That Sinking Feeling*?

13 Who starred in the film of Jessie Kesson's book *Another Time, Another Place*?

14 What real event provided the inspiration for *Whisky Galore*?

15 What role did Robert Carlyle play in *Trainspotting*?

16 Which fondly remembered Scottish actor appeared in *The Great Escape*, *Whisky Galore*, *The Prime of Miss Jean Brodie* and *Mutiny on the Bounty*?

17 Name the Scots actor who starred in *Star Wars: The Phantom Menace*.

18 Who wrote the book upon which the film *The Big Man* is based?

19 Which Scots actor won an Academy Award for his part in *The Untouchables*?

20 Which Scottish hero was played in a film by Liam Neeson?

21 Which Scots actor was chosen to play the part of Hagrid in the film versions of the *Harry Potter* books?

22 Who wrote the book upon which the film *Ring of Bright Water* is based?

23 Who played Gregory in *Gregory's Girl*?

24 Which fictional Edinburgh schoolteacher was played by Maggie Smith in an Academy Award winning film?

25 Which book by Compton Mackenzie was made into a film?

Answers: p150

The Borders

1   Which famous publishing family is associated with Peebles?
2   Who founded Melrose Abbey?
3   Which two architects were involved in the design of Floors Castle?
4   Where are Priorwood Gardens?
5   On which two rivers is the town of Kelso situated?
6   In which Borders castle did Malcolm IV die?
7   Which castle was used in the filming of *Greystoke*?
8   In which park are the Jedburgh Border Games held each year?
9   In which town is the Cornice Museum of Ornamental Plasterwork?
10 In which month is the Hawick Common Riding held?
11 What is housed in Gala House?
12 Which Borders fishing port suffered terrible losses to its fishing fleet in a storm in 1881?
13 Which Borders town celebrates the Braw Lads Gathering every year?
14 Which famous Scottish poet was born in Ettrick?
15 Which wizard is said to have split the Eildon Hills from one hill into three?
16 Which famous racing driver grew up in the village of Duns?
17 In which century was the original priory at Coldingham founded?
18 Near which Borders town are Kailzie Gardens?
19 How many arches are there in the bridge over the Tweed at Kelso?
20 Near which Borders town is Ferniehurst Castle?
21 Which abbey was the largest of those built in the Borders?
22 On the roof of which Borders abbey can a pig be seen be seen playing the bagpipes?
23 Where is St Ronan's Well?
24 Which Borders abbey was founded by Hugo de Morville?
25 Where are the ruins of Tinnis Castle?

Answers: p151

1   In which decade was education for all children between the ages of 5 and 13 made compulsory in Scotland?
2   What crisis hit Scotland in 1622–23, particularly in the Highlands?
3   During which king's reign was Mons Meg brought to Britain?
4   What disease spread through Scotland around 1350?
5   For what purpose was the Kelvingrove Museum and Art Gallery first built?
6   In which century were potatoes first grown in Scotland?
7   Where did George IV first wear a kilt?
8   What is the EICC?
9   What anniversary of Scottish history fell in April 1996?
10 What was the name of the first lighthouse built in Scotland?
11 Which Scottish nobleman was sued unsuccessfully by Oscar Wilde?
12 What is the name of the man whose execution sparked off the Porteous Riots?
13 Name Glasgow's second university which was established through the amalgamation of the Royal College of Science and Technology and the Scottish College of Commerce.
14 Name the Scots husband of Amy Johnson who crossed the Atlantic with her in 1933.
15 George MacLeod is remembered as the founder of the Iona Community. In which sphere of political action was he also very much involved?
16 Where is the Scottish home of Paul McCartney?
17 What profession did poet Norman McCaig follow?
18 Where was Eric Liddell born?
19 Where is David Livingstone buried?
20 How many times did John Knox marry?
21 Who published memoirs entitled *Roamin' in the Gloamin'*?
22 What is the name of the dancer who married Ludovic Kennedy?
23 The first known film footage made in Scotland featured whom, and where?
24 What is the name of the artist who used to own the island of Eigg?
25 Who was responsible for managing Homecoming Scotland 2009?

Answers: p151

Industry 2

1   What brought hopes of wealth and prosperity to the Cononish Estate near Tyndrum for a while in the 1990s?
2   What industry is the biggest private employer in Orkney?
3   In which year did a sodium-cooled fast reactor go on fire at Dounreay?
4   Name the Scot who was first director-general of the Concorde Project.
5   What kind of industry was established by Thomas Nelson in Edinburgh in the late nineteenth century?
6   In which century was the booksellers, John Smith, founded?
7   Where was the first Chamber of Commerce in Britain founded?
8   Where was the oldest coal mine in Scotland?
9   What used to be mined on the island of Luing?
10 Who founded the New Lanark Twist Company?
11 When was the Clydesdale Banking Company founded?
12 When was the STUC formed?
13 Where did Scotland's worst pit disaster take place?
14 Who wrote *A General View of the Coal Trade of Scotland* in 1808?
15 What was the season for Scottish herring fishing?
16 How were herring caught?
17 What disastrous occurrences hit Scottish farming in 1836 and 1846?
18 What kind of decorative product is associated with Caithness?
19 When were the post offices of England and Scotland united?
20 When was The Highlands and Islands Development Board set up?
21 In which industry was Alexander McDonald a leader of the workers in the nineteenth century?
22 In which decade was the Institute of Bankers of Scotland formed?
23 Which bank was formed in 1695?
24 Where did J. & P. Coats base their business in Scotland?
25 Where was the SCWS formed?

Answers: p152

Royalty

1   Which member of the present royal family holds the title of Lord of the Isles?
2   Who was David II's father?
3   In what year was Charles I executed?
4   Who was the mother of Mary, Queen of Scots?
5   To whom was the Maid of Norway betrothed?
6   In what year was James III born?
7   Where did James V die?
8   Which Scottish king was killed at the Battle of Flodden?
9   Who was the last Stewart on the throne?
10 Which king was the grandson of David I?
11 In what year did the young Mary, Queen of Scots, arrive back in Scotland from France?
12 How did James II die?
13 Who was the mother of James V?
14 Which king boasted that he ruled Scotland with his pen?
15 What was the name of Macbeth's wife?
16 In what year did James VI become king of both Scotland and England?
17 Which king was crowned at Holyrood in 1633?
18 When did James VII ascend the throne?
19 What relation was William of Orange to James VII?
20 Who acted as regent in James V's minority?
21 How old was James IV when he became king?
22 Whom did James VI marry?
23 Which Scottish monarch was killed when his horse threw him over a cliff?
24 Where was Bonnie Prince Charlie born?
25 Which Scottish king was murdered in 1437?

Answers: p152

Football 1

1 When was the Scottish First Division Championship superseded by the Premier Division Championship?

2 Which football club has won the First/Premier Division Championship the most times since 1891?

3 Which team won the European Cup in 1967?

4 Who was the celebrated Scottish manager of Manchester United for over 20 years?

5 How many caps did Kenny Dalglish win for Scotland?

6 For what reason was the FA Cup withdrawn in 1909?

7 In which season did Third Lanark win the First Division Championship?

8 How many times did Rangers win the First Division between 1900 and 1950?

9 In what year was the FA Cup renamed the Tennants Cup?

10 With which English team is the name of former Scottish footballer Dennis Law associated?

11 Which football team is known as 'the Jags'?

12 Which football team plays at Easter Road?

13 With whom does Dennis Law share his record of most goals scored for his country?

14 In which year was Dundee United founded?

15 Who was the manager of the Lisbon Lions?

16 Who are 'the Bankies'?

17 Which Scottish player scored the winning goal for Liverpool in the European Cup Final of 1978?

18 Which team won the 2009 Scottish Cup Final?

19 Name the famous football manager who was born in Govan in 1941.

20 What are the colours of the Kilmarnock football team?

21 Which team beat Rangers in a replay in the final of the 1905 FA Cup?

22 Which former England captain was assistant coach to the Scotland team in 2009?

23 During which World War was Scottish Football League competition suspended?

24 Which team is affectionately known as 'the Jam Tarts'?

25 Which is the biggest football stadium in Scotland?

Answers: p153

1   What is the name of the RSPB nature reserve on the shores of Loch Leven?
2   What is the name by which the vast areas of woodland which once covered much of Scotland are known?
3   What is an SSSI?
4   Which two Scottish islands were joined by a causeway in 2000?
5   Where is Scotland's only *natural* World Heritage Site?
6   Who/what were Megan and Morag?
7   Where is the east end of the Southern Upland Way?
8   Why have the villages of East Wemyss and West Wemyss needed government funding for their own protection?
9   What is Scotland's only native breed of hunting dog?
10 Which Scottish female singer was awarded an OBE for her services to music in 2000?
11 Which popular TV series was filmed in the Badenoch/Newtonmore area?
12 Edinburgh-born man, Richard Tait, invented the fastest-selling board game in history. What is it called?
13 Where is Scotland's first 'Booktown'?
14 Which king introduced the feudal system to Scotland?
15 For how many years was Mary, Queen of Scots, kept in captivity by Elizabeth I of England?
16 With which football club is the name of Ebbe Skovdahl associated?
17 Name the former Scottish politician who published a book entitled *Imagine*.
18 Which landmark in Ireland is similar in geology to the island of Staffa?
19 Who sponsors the 'Spirit of Scotland' awards?
20 In which decade did soldier, diplomat and historian, Fitzroy Maclean, die?
21 What was the trade of Kirkpatrick Macmillan?
22 Which famous criminal case featured in Ludovic Kennedy's *A Presumption of Innocence*?
23 Which well-known firm of Edinburgh booksellers was founded in 1848?
24 Who was the brother of the Wolf of Badenoch?
25 The name of which Scottish loch is associated with kippers?

Answers: p153

Art

1   Which artist painted many beautiful scenes of the coast at Catterline?
2   With which type of painting is Sir Henry Raeburn associated?
3   What relation was Allan Ramsay, painter, to the poet of the same name?
4   Name the contemporary Scottish painter who produced a series of pictures while in hospital recovering from a liver transplant.
5   Which Scottish sculptor is associated with the question mark?
6   What was the name by which Fergusson, Cadell, Peploe and Hunter were known collectively?
7   Which Scottish artist and writer transformed his home into 'Little Sparta'?
8   In which city is the Scottish National Portrait Gallery?
9   Which Scottish artist was appointed Britain's war artist in Bosnia?
10 Who painted *The Porteous Mob* in 1855?
11 Where did William Gillies study art?
12 With which group of painters is the name of James Guthrie associated?
13 Who became head of the Glasgow School of Art in 1885?
14 What was the name of Charles Rennie Mackintosh's artist wife?
15 Who painted *The Indian Rug*?
16 Which contemporary artist painted a series of murals for the People's Palace in Glasgow?
17 He was a painter working at the end of the nineteenth century, who produced energetic and powerful seascapes, such as *The Storm*. Who was he?
18 Which painter succeeded Raeburn as the king's official artist?
19 Name the Italo-Scottish sculptor and printmaker who was a pioneer of Pop Art.
20 Where are the Phoebe Anna Traquair murals to be found?
21 With which group of artists were Margaret Macdonald, Frances Macdonald, Jessie Newbery and Jessie King associated?
22 Which Scots artist was known for his paintings of fairies?
23 Which centre on the northeast coast of Scotland promotes interest in glass as an art form?
24 Broughton House, Kirkcudbright was once the home of which artist?
25 Which famous Scottish cartoonist and caricaturist died in 1997?

Answers: p154

Dumfries & Galloway

1   Near which town is the castle of Drumlanrig?
2   Where did Robert the Bruce stab the Red Comyn?
3   Which town is the smallest royal burgh in Scotland?
4   In which year did the Lockerbie air disaster occur?
5   What stands on the Colvin Fountain in Moffat?
6   Near which town is the Craigleuch Explorers' Museum?
7   What is the name of the artist E.A. Hornel's former home in Kirkcudbright?
8   In which century was Glenluce Abbey founded?
9   Which textile industry once flourished in Gatehouse of Fleet?
10 On the estuary of which river is Kippford situated?
11 In which abbey (now ruined) in Dumfries and Galloway did Mary, Queen of Scots, spend her last night in Scotland?
12 On which river is St John's Town of Dalry situated?
13 In which village were Covenanting declarations made in 1680 and 1685?
14 In which century was the Castle of St John in Stranraer built?
15 Where is the Monreith Cross?
16 How many Wigtown Martyrs were there?
17 Where was Kirkpatrick Macmillan, inventor of the bicycle, born?
18 Where is the Stewartry Museum?
19 In which churchyard is Robert Burns buried?
20 Which castle near Castle Douglas was a stronghold of the Douglas family?
21 In which village was William Paterson, founder of the Bank of England, born?
22 Where is the second-oldest subscription library in Great Britain?
23 What is 'the White Coomb'?
24 Near which town is Craigcaffie Castle situated?
25 In which village was Thomas Carlyle born?

Answers: p154

Sport 1

1   Which swimmer won an Olympic gold medal for the 200-metre breaststroke in 1976?
2   Name the Scottish racing driver who was world champion in 1971.
3   Which Scottish runner became the oldest winner of the 100-metre sprint in the Olympic Games in 1980?
4   In which year was Bill McLaren awarded the Freedom of Scottish Rugby?
5   Name the Scottish racing driver and former world champion who was born in 1936.
6   With which sport is the name of Willie Auchterlonie associated?
7   Where was the Millennium British Open Golf Championship held?
8   With which sport is the name of Benny Lynch associated?
9   In which month of the year is the Ben Nevis Hill Race traditionally held?
10   Which world-class Scottish snooker player was born in Edinburgh in 1969?
11   Who was the first Scot to become World Rally Champion?
12   Which sport do the Scottish Claymores play?
13   Which Scottish golfer won the British Open in 1985?
14   Which Scottish jockey won the Derby in 1979 on Troy?
15   Which Scot won the 1999 British Open?
16   Name the gold medal-winning Scots yachtswoman of the 2000 and 2004 Olympics.
17   Who made the fastest female marathon debut in the New York Marathon in 1991?
18   In which athletics event did Alan Wells compete before he took up sprinting?
19   With which Edinburgh swimming club did David Wilkie train?
20   When was Stewart Grand Prix sold to Ford?
21   In 2008, which Scottish rugby international broke the record held by Andy Irvine for point-scoring for Scotland in international matches?
22   Who became the youngest-ever winner of the Embassy World Snooker Championship in 1990?
23   Where did Alex Ferguson begin his career as a football manager?
24   How many gold medals did Chris Hoy win for cycling in the 2008 Beijing Olympic Games?
25   In which year was Kenny Dalglish asked to manage Liverpool?

Answers: p155

General Knowledge 12

1   In which decade was the SYHA formed?
2   Where is Robert Adam buried?
3   In which decade did the first postage stamps come into use in Scotland?
4   On which foreign island did Alexander Selkirk survive alone for more than four years?
5   What was the real name of Kinmont Willie?
6   By which name was James Crichton of Eliock, the sixteenth-century scholar, also known?
7   In which century was the first Bible printed in Scotland?
8   In which century did General Wade come to Scotland?
9   What is the name of the largest teachers' union in Scotland?
10 What are the titles of the two Law Officers of the Crown?
11 In which decade were the Reith Lectures instituted?
12 What relationship did John Playfair bear to William Playfair?
13 What Nobel Prize did James Mirrlees win in 1996?
14 Name the Scot who produced the first waterproof cloth.
15 At which exhibition did Margaret Macdonald, wife of Charles Rennie Mackintosh, win a Diploma of Honour in 1902?
16 In which country was Scots medical pioneer, Elsie Inglis, born?
17 Which one was the younger: obstetrician, William Hunter, or his surgeon brother, John?
18 What was the profession of David Octavius Hill, 1802–70?
19 Who was goldsmith to James VI and Anne of Denmark?
20 When did the first Edinburgh Military Tattoo take place?
21 Which mountains were put up for sale by John Macleod in 2000?
22 In which year did an explosion take place in a waste shaft at Dounreay?
23 Which agricultural event takes place at Ingliston every year in June?
24 What is the name of the construction firm started by George Balfour in 1909?
25 In which year did John Balliol make his claim to the Scottish throne?

Answers: p155

Music 2

1   What is a 'clarsach'?
2   What was the name of the first chart hit for the Scottish band Texas?
3   What is the name of the young musician from West Kilbride who was named BBC Young Musician of the Year in 2004?
4   Which French composer wrote *Chanson Ecossaise*?
5   What is the name for the characteristic rhythmic figure found in Strathspey music?
6   Who wrote the Scottish anthem, 'Flower of Scotland'?
7   Of which musical duo was the composer of 'Flower of Scotland' one half?
8   What is mouth music?
9   Jimmy Shand was known worldwide for his music. What instrument did he play?
10 What do the Proclaimers have in common with Jimmy Shand?
11 Who was the Scot responsible, along with Bob Geldof, for the launch of Live Aid in 1985?
12 How many drones do Scottish bagpipes have?
13 What is the time signature of reel music?
14 Which band had a hit with 'Thorn in my Side'?
15 Which musical organization was founded by Sir Alexander Gibson?
16 What kind of music did John Riddell compose?
17 Who wrote *The Art of Touching the Keyboard*?
18 Niel Gow's skills as a fiddle player and songwriter are still recognized nearly two hundred years after his death. Where was he born?
19 Which popular Scottish tenor was born in 1927?
20 What instrument did Helen Hopekirk play?
21 Name the Scottish pop group whose version of 'Love is All Around' featured in the film *Four Weddings and a Funeral*.
22 Which Scottish singer sang 'A Scottish Soldier'?
23 Which German composer wrote *The Scottish Symphony*, inspired by a visit to Holyrood?
24 Name the concerto written by Max Bruch, based on Scottish tunes.
25 What instrument does Shetland musician Aly Bain play?

Answers: p156

Islands of Scotland

1   What is the name given to the line of islands stretching from Barra Head to Butt of Lewis?
2   Where is Eilan Glas Lighthouse?
3   Barra is the seat of which clan?
4   In what year was the island of St Kilda abandoned?
5   What is the magical heirloom kept in Dunvegan Castle?
6   On which island can you find 'the Singing Sands'?
7   What is the capital of Orkney?
8   Where on Mull does the ferry from Oban land?
9   What island inspired Mendelssohn to write *The Hebridean Overture*?
10 On which island is Prince Charlie's Cave?
11 What is the island port of North Uist?
12 What sport can you play on Arinagour on Coll?
13 Where is St Oran's Chapel?
14 Where is Bowmore?
15 On which island is the Clan Donald Centre?
16 Where on Mull is the Mull Little Theatre?
17 The Thrushel Stone is the largest single stone in Scotland. Where is it?
18 What is the name of the castle in Castlebay Harbour?
19 What is the name of the highest peak on South Uist?
20 What is the man-made landmark on the Butt of Lewis?
21 What is the name of the gardeners' paradise on the island of Gigha?
22 Where did George Orwell write *1984*?
23 What is the name of the home of the Dukes of Hamilton on Arran?
24 What is the most northerly island of Orkney?
25 What is Scapa Flow famous for?

Answers: p156

Great Scots 2

1   Which philosopher and historian wrote an *Essay on the History of Civil Society* in 1767?

2   Which Scottish politician of the early twentieth century spent some time working as a rancher in South America?

3   Which Scottish writer and broadcaster wrote *Euthanasia: the Good Death*?

4   Name the poet and writer who published *The Brownie of Bodsbeck* in the nineteenth century.

5   Name the Scottish theologian who published *Institutes of Theology*.

6   Which anaesthetic did James Young Simpson introduce into midwifery?

7   Name the Scottish lawyer and writer who published *Jus Feudale* in 1608.

8   Name the Scottish painter and King's Limner in Scotland who was knighted in 1836.

9   What is the name of the journal founded by Scots philosopher and psychologist Alexander Bain?

10   In which occupation was Lord Reith originally trained?

11   What is the name of the Scots theologian who published his own translation of the New Testament in 1968?

12   Name the Scottish football manager who began his management career with Dunfermline Athletic.

13   Name the motor-racing hero who received a knighthood in the Queen's Birthday Honours List in 2001.

14   What was the profession of John Boyd Dunlop?

15   Name the Scottish barrister who published *Eve Was Framed*.

16   Which famous Scot became an outlaw after being accused of embezzling money from the Duke of Montrose?

17   Which Scottish physicist wrote *An Elementary Treatise on Rational Mechanics*?

18   What is the name of the Scottish lexicographer who edited a large part of the *New English Dictionary*, which later became the *Oxford English Dictionary*?

19   With which branch of learning is James Clerk Maxwell's name associated?

20   What was the profession of Nobel Prize winner Sir William Ramsay?

21   Of which institution was Lord George Thomson of Monifieth the chairman from 1981 to 1988?

22   Name the Scottish obstetrician who became physician to the Queen in Scotland in 1847.

23   Which nationalistic poet has been called 'the Voice of Scotland'?

24   Name the Scots scientist who, in conjunction with Lord John Rayleigh, discovered argon.

25   Which eminent Scottish bacteriologist worked as a shipping clerk before taking up medicine?

Answers: p157

QUESTIONS

59

General Knowledge 13

1 Where is the world's largest colony of gannets to be found?
2 Who does Charlie's Monument in Coldstream honour?
3 Where is the start of the Southern Upland Way?
4 How many lambs did Dolly the sheep have altogether?
5 By what name did Arthur Stanley Jefferson become famous?
6 Where was BBC Radio Tweed based?
7 For what purpose would 'a bannock stane' be used?
8 Which novel by Sir Walter Scott features Jinglin' Geordie?
9 In which decade was the North Bridge in Edinburgh built?
10 What would 'a targe' be used for?
11 Which objects were sometimes given the nickname 'black breeks'?
12 What is a 'souter'?
13 Which prime minister of Great Britain encouraged the raising of Highland regiments to fight for the British government?
14 Whose murder is described in *Kidnapped*?
15 What was the *Yellow Carvel*?
16 During which king's reign did Berwick finally become an English town?
17 In which decade was the General Teaching Council of Scotland established?
18 How are the Law Officers of the Crown selected?
19 Where was the first Bible printed in Scotland?
20 In which year was Lord Darnley murdered?
21 What is 'Hunt the Gowk'?
22 What was the name given to the mythical giant of the Eildon Hills?
23 Which sculptor created *Straw Locomotive* and *Paper Boat*?
24 In which century was the Boys' Brigade founded?
25 'Some people think that football is a matter of life and death. I don't like that attitude. I can assure them it is much more serious than that.' Who said this?

Answers: p157

Castles

1 Where is Scalloway Castle?

2 Dunrobin Castle is the seat of which noble Scottish family?

3 What is special about Caerlaverock Castle?

4 Which Scottish mathematician's family once owned Lauriston Castle in Edinburgh?

5 Which family owned Hailes Castle in East Lothian in the fourteenth century?

6 Which castle near Elie in Fife is now part of an exclusive timeshare development?

7 For which family was Castle Tioram built?

8 For which purpose is Carbisdale Castle now used?

9 Where did the Black Dinner of 1440 take place?

10 To which famous Edinburgh benefactor did Lennox Castle belong?

11 In which castle did Robert III die?

12 To which castle did Mary, Queen of Scots, go immediately after her escape from Loch Leven?

13 Of which castle was the Goblin Ha' a part?

14 Which family owns Roslin Castle in Lothian?

15 What kind of ghost is said to haunt Abergeldie Castle in Deeside?

16 Which family owns Cortachy Castle in Angus?

17 From which century does MacLellan's Castle in Kirkcudbright date?

18 Name the castle near North Berwick which was built in the fourteenth century by William, 1st Earl of Douglas.

19 Near which town is Castle Campbell?

20 On which island is Muness Castle?

21 Where is Kisimul Castle?

22 Who was responsible for the restoration of Duart Castle on Mull?

23 Which castle near Castle Douglas once belonged to Archibald the Grim?

24 Where is Dunvegan Castle?

25 In which century was the present Balmoral Castle built?

Answers: p158

Literature 2

1   Who created Dr Jekyll and Mr Hyde?

2   Who wrote *My Schools and Schoolmasters* in 1852?

3   Who wrote *A Window in Thrums*?

4   Which nineteenth-century Scottish novelist wrote *The Annals of the Parish* and *The Provost*?

5   Whose autobiography, *Brave Days*, was published in 1931?

6   Where was Scots writer Jessie Kesson born?

7   Which Scots writer was 1st Baron Tweedsmuir?

8   Name the author of *At the Back of the North Wind* and *The Princess and the Curdie*.

9   Who wrote *The Big Man*?

10 Name the author of *Tunes of Glory*.

11 Which contemporary Scottish writer won the Macallan Golden Dagger for Fiction for his novel *Black and Blue*?

12 Who wrote *Tales of a Grandfather*?

13 Who published the first collection of the Waverley novels?

14 Fanny, the wife of Robert Louis Stevenson, burned the first draft of one of his books because she did not think it would be a success. Which book was it?

15 What is the Ashestiel Manuscript?

16 In which year was the New Testament first published in Gaelic?

17 Who wrote *The Grey Coast*?

18 Which Scottish literary magazine was started in 1817?

19 In which decade was *Chambers's Journal* started?

20 Laura Jackson is a successful and respected biographer of celebrities such as Brian Jones and Ewan McGregor. Where in Scotland does she live?

21 What is the name of the man who writes under the pseudonym of Ian Hay?

22 In which trade did novelist James Kelman originally train?

23 Which dictionary publisher in Edinburgh closed down in 2009?

24 Who wrote a *History of Scottish Literature* in 1977?

25 Which novel by George Orwell was largely written on the the island of Jura?

Answers: p158

Scottish Women

1. What was Mary Slessor's job before she became a missionary?
2. For which constituency did Katharine, Duchess of Atholl, become MP in 1923?
3. Which Scottish soprano became director of the Chicago Grand Opera?
4. Which Scottish writer wrote the autobiographical work *Curriculum Vitae*?
5. Who founded the Scottish Women's Suffragette Federation?
6. In which race did Liz McColgan win a silver medal at the Olympic games in Seoul?
7. How did Miranda Barry achieve her ambition to train as a surgeon?
8. What profession did Liz Lochhead follow before she became a writer?
9. When was Winnie Ewing first elected to the European parliament?
10. What parliamentary position did Helen Liddell hold at the time of the 2001 general election?
11. Which Scottish actress starred in the 1970s TV comedy *My Wife Next Door*?
12. Alison Ramsay received an MBE in 2001 for her sporting achievements for Scotland and Great Britain. At which sport did she achieve excellence?
13. Name the Scottish woman who was composer-in-residence at the RSAM from 1988 to 1991.
14. How many husbands did Mary, Queen of Scots, have?
15. Whom did Scots singer Annie Lennox partner in the Eurythmics?
16. Name the woman whose face became famous in TV adverts for her family's soup.
17. Where was barrister Helena Kennedy born?
18. Which Scottish woman started a riot in 1637?
19. Which Scottish painter was the first woman to become a full member of both the RSA and the RA?
20. In which year was Evelyn Glennie born?
21. Which woman ran an inn in the Borders with famous literary connections?
22. Which famous Scottish songwriter wrote a collection of songs that were published after her death as *Lays of Strathearn*?
23. Which Scottish actress starred in the film *From Here to Eternity*?
24. In which century was St Margaret canonized?
25. Name the woman who attempted to ski to the North Pole unsupported in 1969?

Answers: p159

General Knowledge 14

1 What did the Physic Garden in Edinburgh eventually become?
2 What was the name of Robert II's mother?
3 Whose autobiography is entitled *Wearing Spurs*?
4 In which decade was the Ballachulish Bridge built?
5 Which Labour politician won the Nobel Peace Prize in 1934?
6 Which eminent Scot was the deputy chief prosecutor at the Nuremberg Trials?
7 Name the Scot who was Chancellor of the Exchequer under John Major from 1990 to 1993.
8 Where did Charles I surrender to the English forces in 1646?
9 What relationship did Malcolm III bear to Duncan I?
10 Who was Lord High Chancellor of Great Britain from 1987 to 1997?
11 Which prize was awarded to John MacLeod in 1923?
12 What is the middle name of the author Iain Banks?
13 How did Dame Isobel Baillie become famous?
14 In which century was Arthur James Balfour, 1st Earl of Balfour, Chief Secretary for Northern Ireland?
15 What was the name of the open-air swimming pool at Macduff?
16 Whose death sparked off the Wars of Independence in Scotland?
17 Who was known as 'the Scottish Hogarth'?
18 In which year did the last lighthouse keeper in Scotland leave his post as automation took over?
19 In which year did PM Gordon Brown marry?
20 Which Scottish school did Prince Phillip, Prince Charles and Prince Andrew attend?
21 Which site in Edinburgh becomes a 'winter wonderland' at Christmas?
22 Who was the first Scottish king to issue his own autonomous coinage?
23 In which century was the last wild boar in Scotland hunted down?
24 What title did James VII hold before he became king?
25 When was universal male suffrage granted in Scotland?

Answers: p159

Around & About in Scotland 2

1 By which Moray town can you see Sueno's Stone?
2 Where is James III buried?
3 Where is Barra Castle?
4 Where is the Branklyn Garden?
5 In which city is Lady Stair's House?
6 Where can you visit the Dynamic Earth Exhibition?
7 Where can you see a royal tennis court?
8 Near which village in East Lothian is Hailes Castle?
9 Where is the best-preserved broch in Scotland and what is its name?
10 Where is Loch Brittle?
11 In which Scottish burgh is Madras College?
12 Where are the Falls of Lora?
13 For which town was the Stanely Reservoir created?
14 What is Neptune's Staircase, and where is it?
15 Where is the Innerpeffray Library?
16 Where is the Devil's Beeftub?
17 Near which town is the Glenmorangie Distillery?
18 Where in Scotland can you walk along the Khyber Pass?
19 Which Scottish island was host to *Bacillus anthracis* from 1942 to 1987?
20 Where is the Scottish Fisheries Museum?
21 In which group of islands is the island of Fetlar?
22 Where can you visit the David Livingstone Centre?
23 Where are the Falls of Glomach?
24 What is the Pineapple and where is it?
25 Where is the Devil's Staircase?

Answers: p160

Science, Engineering, Invention & Innovation

1 What was the name of George Stephenson's famous locomotive?

2 In which year was the telephone invented by Alexander Graham Bell?

3 Who was the Scot who designed the Bell Rock Lighthouse?

4 What was invented by Robert William Thomson?

5 Who invented the first duplicating machine?

6 Which father and son were responsible for the design and construction of London Bridge?

7 When was Thomas Telford born?

8 Which Scot first produced pneumatic tyres commercially?

9 Who patented the double engine?

10 With which invention is Sir David Brewster associated?

11 Who invented the oscillating engine?

12 Who built the first pedal bicycle?

13 Which invention is attributed both to Charles Tennant and Charles Macintosh?

14 What was the measurement chosen by George Stephenson, still in use, for the distance between rails?

15 Who pioneered the manufacturing of paraffin in Scotland?

16 Who invented the rotary press?

17 Where was Dolly, the first cloned sheep, born?

18 Who proposed the absolute temperature scale (named after him)?

19 What was the *Charlotte Dundas*?

20 Who discovered the magneto-optic effect?

21 Who was the leader of the team which cloned Dolly, the sheep?

22 Why was Frostie the calf so named?

23 In which year did John Logie Baird give the first demonstration of television?

24 What invention by Ian Donald did much to improve antenatal care for women and their babies?

25 Who invented the patent still?

Answers: p160

Fife

1   In which century was the East Neuk town of Crail granted status as a royal burgh?

2   Whose remains were discovered and then re-interred in Dunfermline Abbey in the early nineteenth century?

3   In which Fife seaside town is the Lady's Tower?

4   At the foot of which hills does the town of Falkland stand?

5   Name the airforce base in Fife which hosts a major air show.

6   Which village is situated beneath the north end of the Forth Railway Bridge?

7   Where is St Fillan's Cave?

8   In which Fife town is St Rule's Tower?

9   Which two industries, apart from fishing, were once associated with St Monans?

10   In which Fife town is St Mungo's Chapel?

11   Name Fife's new town and centre of light industry.

12   In which town is Pittencrieff Park?

13   With which industry is Mossmorran associated?

14   From which century does the castle at Aberdour date?

15   What is housed in St Ayles' Land in Anstruther?

16   Where is the nearest railway station to St Andrews?

17   Which textile industry once flourished in the town of Dunfermline?

18   In which town in Fife did James V die?

19   Near which town in Fife is Scotland's 'Secret Bunker'?

20   In which town in Fife might you take a walk along the Lade Braes?

21   In days when corporal punishment was still permitted in schools, to which town in Fife might a teacher go to buy a new tawse?

22   Which fishing town in Fife has a windmill?

23   Which Scottish monarch was thrown from his horse at Kinghorn?

24   In which historic Fife town is Stinking Wynd?

25   By which Fife burgh is Kincraig Point?

Answers: p161

General Knowledge 15

1. In which king's reign did Somerled, Lord of Argyll, attack Glasgow?
2. Where was *The Great Michael* built?
3. After which battle in 1644 did Montrose take Perth?
4. Which Scottish airport was attacked by terrorists in 2007?
5. Which Scot was made chairman and chief executive of British Telecom in 1985?
6. Which flower was the emblem of the '45 Jacobites?
7. Which Scottish soap featured Mrs Mac?
8. Which Edinburgh publisher was named as publisher of the year in 2003?
9. In which century was the Scottish Fisheries Commission established?
10. What were Lochaber stones used for all over Scotland?
11. Where was Cardinal Thomas Winning born?
12. Where was the first purpose-built mosque in Scotland built?
13. Where did boxer, Jim Watt, become world champion?
14. In the 1970s 'I found it at Bruce's' was the slogan for what kind of business?
15. In which decade did Scottish miners finally become free men?
16. In the nineteenth century, which Scottish university had the largest number of students?
17. Who went on strike throughout Scotland in 1812?
18. Who wrote *Journals and Memorials of His Time*?
19. Which political activist was tried for sedition in 1918?
20. With which author is the character of 'Wee Jakie' associated?
21. Which serial killer famously conducted his own defence at his murder trial in 1958?
22. With which island is the name of St Molaise associated?
23. What is the name of the trust established in 1984, to acquire wild land in Great Britain?
24. Whom did Thomas Reid succeed as professor of moral philosophy at Glasgow University in 1764?
25. In which year did the Porteous Riots take place?

Answers: p161

Where Were They Born?

QUESTIONS

1   Robert Adam, architect
2   Alexander Selkirk, sailor
3   Neil Munro, novelist
4   John Knox, Protestant reformer
5   Robert the Bruce, king
6   Mary, Queen of Scots
7   John Buchan, novelist
8   Chris Hoy, cyclist
9   James Ramsay MacDonald, Prime Minister
10 Alex Gray, crime writer
11 Adam Smith, economist
12 Alexander Graham Bell, inventor
13 Sir Alex Ferguson, football manager
14 Lord Francis Jeffrey, judge
15 David Livingstone, missionary and explorer
16 James Young Simpson, obstetrician
17 Sir Walter Scott, writer
18 Ian Rankin, crime writer
19 Charles Rennie Mackintosh, architect
20 J.M. Barrie, novelist
21 Andrew Murray, tennis player
22 James VI
23 James Boswell, writer
24 Hugh MacDiarmid, poet
25 Andrew Carnegie, millionaire philanthropist

Answers: p162

Otherwise Known As . . .

1. By which name did Christopher Murray Grieve become famous?
2. What is Lulu's real name?
3. Who was Robert Burns's 'Highland Mary'?
4. Who was known as 'the Scottish Samurai'?
5. Which town was known in fiction as 'Thrums'?
6. Which town in Fife is known as 'the Auld Grey Toun'?
7. Who was 'the Wisest Fool in Christendom'?
8. Who was 'the Red Fox'?
9. Who was known as 'the Strathspey King'?
10. Who was 'Jinglin' Geordie'?
11. Which town in Aberdeenshire is also known as 'Gamrie'?
12. Which king of Scotland was known as 'the Maiden'?
13. By which name was Malcolm III known?
14. Which Fife town has been called 'the Lang Toun'?
15. Which footballer was known as 'Slim Jim'?
16. Which Scottish town is known as 'the Honest Toun'?
17. Which king was known as 'the Lion'?
18. Who was known as 'Toom Tabard'?
19. Which writer was known as 'the Wizard of the North'?
20. Who were 'the Famous Five'?
21. Who is 'the Voice of Scottish Rugby'?
22. Who was 'the Hammer of the Scots'?
23. What was the Thin Red Line?
24. Who was known as 'Bell-the-Cat'?
25. Who was 'Bluidy Mackenzie'

Answers: p162

Films & Film Stars 2

1   Which famous Scot played James Bond?

2   Which Scottish city hosts an international film festival?

3   Name the Scots actor who bared his all in the film *The Full Monty*.

4   Which Scots actor and comedian starred in *Nuns on the Run*?

5   In which box-office sell-out did Scottish actor John Hannah recite a poem by W.H. Auden?

6   Which village in the north-east was used as a backdrop for the film *Local Hero*?

7   Who played the prison officer in the television comedy *Porridge* and also had a major role in the film *Local Hero*?

8   Which Scottish actor co-starred with Pauline Collins in *Shirley Valentine*?

9   Where was *Trainspotting* set?

10 Name the Scots comedian who co-starred with Judi Dench in *Mrs Brown*.

11 Where is the beach that features in the opening sequence of *Chariots of Fire*?

12 What is the name of the film that is based on the life of Jimmy Boyle?

13 Which Scots film actor, who died in 1976, played a leading role in *The Belles of St Trinian's* (1954)?

14 Which Scots actor co-starred with Dirk Bogarde in the *Doctor* films?

15 Who was the Scottish director of *Trainspotting*?

16 When was *Tunes of Glory* made?

17 Who played the Scots missionary Eric Liddell in *Chariots of Fire*?

18 Who was the Scots star of *A Life Less Ordinary*?

19 Name the Scots comedian who played a serious role in the film *Gorky Park*.

20 Which Scots entertainer had a role in *Elstree Calling* in 1930?

21 In which Harry Potter film were Glen Coe and Glenfinnan used as film locations?

22 Name the Scots comedian, entertainer and actor who made his first film appearance in *Geordie* in 1956?

23 Who made a film entitled *Comrades*?

24 Which famous part did Robert Powell, Robert Donat and Kenneth More play in separate film versions of a popular thriller?

25 Name the Scots-born documentary maker who made *Drifters* and *Housing Problems* and who set up the National Film Board of Canada.

Answers: p163

General Knowledge 16

1   To which prominent Scot was Mary Somerville married?
2   Who designed the equestrian statue of the Duke of Wellington in Edinburgh?
3   What should you do with guga?
4   What is the name for the feral sheep which live on St Kilda?
5   Whom did Jane Beaufort marry?
6   Where is the Centre for Contemporary Art?
7   What do we know the festival of Samhain as?
8   In which year did the Scottish football team first win a game in the World Cup?
9   In which century did the General Assembly of the Church of Scotland, as we know it today, first meet?
10 What was the name of the Bill, passed in 1689, which limited the powers of the monarchy and stated that the monarch must be Protestant?
11 Who issued the First Declaration of Indulgence?
12 For how many years did the Stone of Destiny remain at Westminster?
13 Which conflict ended with the Pacification of Berwick?
14 What was the proper title of Black Agnes?
15 Of which king was it recorded that 'he happinit to be slane'?
16 Which King James of Scotland lived the longest?
17 Where are the highest cliffs in Great Britain?
18 Where would you go to visit the Crannog Centre?
19 Which football club was founded in 1888?
20 Who was accused of murdering Pierre Emile l'Angelier?
21 In which year were the heritable jurisdictions of the clan chiefs abolished?
22 Which by-election did Jim Sillars win in 1988?
23 In which battle in 1545 was Lord Dacre victorious over the Scots?
24 Of which other literary Robert was Robert Burns an admirer?
25 Which Scottish actor became a UN Ambassador in 2004?

Answers: p163

Sport 2

1 What are curling stones traditionally made from?
2 Which Scottish town is known as 'the Home of Golf'?
3 How many players are there in a shinty team?
4 When was the Scottish Mountaineering Club founded?
5 Where was the Silver Bell run?
6 What sport is played by the Fife Flyers and the Perth Panthers?
7 With which sport is Niall Mackenzie associated?
8 Who was world champion motor racing driver in 1969?
9 Name the Scottish footballer and assistant manager who was a regular team leader on BBC TV's *A Question of Sport*.
10 In what year was racing driver Jim Clark killed?
11 Who was knocked out by Aurel Toma in 1938?
12 Name the player from Wishaw who became snooker world champion for the third time in 2009.
13 Which Scot won the women's 10,000 metres gold medal in the Commonwealth games of 1986 and 1990?
14 How many Scottish Grand National winners were there between 1960 and 1980?
15 Which snooker player broke the record for the highest number of consecutive tournament wins in 1990?
16 What is the oldest rowing club in Scotland?
17 Who resigned as chairman of Dundee United in October 2000?
18 Where in Scotland is Britain's longest artificial ski-slope?
19 Where are the most famous Highland Games held each year, attended by the royal family?
20 Which Scot has won the title of Champion Jockey five times?
21 What major event will take place at Gleneagles in 2014?
22 For which team was David Coulthard driving when he won the Australian and Italian Grand Prix in 1997?
23 How many goals did Denis Law score for Scotland?
24 Which Scottish golf club determines the rules of the game?
25 What kind of races take place during West Highland Week?

Answers: p164

Language

1   What is a 'puddock/?
2   What is a 'corbie'?
3   What would you do with a 'bodle' in times gone by?
4   What is your 'thrapple'?
5   'Weel done, Cutty Sark!' cried Tam o' Shanter in the famous poem by Robert Burns. What does 'Cutty Sark' mean?
6   'Sic-like' means 'unwell'. True or false?
7   What does the phrase 'Dinna fash yersel' mean?
8   When you 'flit' from one place to another, are you airborne?
9   What time of day is 'the gloamin'?
10 What does 'clishmaclaver' mean?
11 What is 'glaur'?
12 What are your 'hurdies'?
13 What would you do with 'parritch'?
14 What is a 'whang o' kebbuck'?
15 A 'bummie's bike' is a means of transport. True or false?
16 What are 'queans' and 'loons'?
17 If someone said you had a 'muckle gab', would you be flattered? Why/why not?
18 What is a 'moudiwart'?
19 What kind of artisan would use a 'lapstane'?
20 Would you like to be described as 'couthie'? Why/why not?
21 'There was a cloker, dabbit at a man,
    He dee'd for fear, he dee'd for fear . . .'
    What is a 'cloker'?
22 'As I gaed up the Canongate, and through the Netherbow,
    Four-and-twenty wabsters were swingin' in a tow . . .'
    What is a 'wabster' and what is a 'tow'?
23 What does 'wi' a tyauve' mean?
24 What was a 'doit'?
25 What is the name for the dialect of the area around Aberdeen?

Answers: p164

Around Edinburgh & the Lothians

1   Which famous conservationist was born in Dunbar?
2   Where did the last Scottish Parliament for over 350 years meet in 1646?
3   In which Lothian town is the Knox Academy?
4   Where is the Phantassie Doocote?
5   Which river flows through the village of Pencaitland?
6   Where is the Museum of Flight?
7   Where is the site of St Colm's Abbey?
8   Who founded Roslin Castle?
9   Where is the Lady Victoria Colliery?
10 Where will you find the headquarters of Edinburgh Crystal?
11 Where in East Lothian did a notorious witch trial and burning take place in 1591?
12 In which century was Newbattle Abbey founded?
13 Where in West Lothian did John Knox lead his first Protestant communion?
14 Where is the Lizzie Bryce Roundabout?
15 What is the name of the nature reserve beside Dunbar?
16 Which chapel was used as a filming location in the movie *The Da Vinci Code*?
17 In which castle did Mary, Queen of Scots, and Bothwell take refuge after they were married?
18 Where is 'Little France'?
19 Which famous writer lived for a number of years in Lasswade Cottage?
20 Which industry has left its mark on the landscape around Mid Calder?
21 What is the name of the military barracks at Penicuik?
22 Near which village is Hopetoun House?
23 Which river flows through Bonnyrigg?
24 Where is Pinkie House?
25 Which monarch's name is associated with Carberry Hill?

QUESTIONS

Answers: p165

1   In which century was Barlinnie Prison built?
2   In which century was the Andersonian Institute founded in Glasgow?
3   Who founded the Ben Nevis Observatory?
4   Where were the four quarters of William Wallace sent?
5   What was the name of James Watt's English partner in business?
6   Which Scot found the source of the Blue Nile?
7   In the politics of the past, what did the initials SHRA stand for?
8   Which military unit was founded by Sir Archibald David Stirling?
9   Whom did Graeme Souness succeed as manager of Liverpool in 1991?
10 What were the names of the two clans of the Picts?
11 Which sporting organization was formed in 1873?
12 Which Scottish regiment was raised by the Earl of Leven?
13 Under which monarch was the College of Justice instituted in Scotland?
14 Which town in Berwickshire is associated with the Glasgow School of painters?
15 What title was General Wade given when he came to Scotland?
16 In which century were mail coaches introduced between London and Edinburgh?
17 What is the only English team in the Scottish football league?
18 Where is the Brig o' Doon?
19 What does 'carse' mean?
20 In which part of Scotland was the real Admirable Crichton born?
21 In which year was the Flodden Wall built?
22 What are the names of the characters played which brought fame to Forbes Masson and Alan Cumming?
23 At which Scottish university did Prince William choose to study?
24 Which female Scots TV presenter fronted a popular series in 1991 about the Munros?
25 What are the names of Glasgow's two main railway stations?

Answers: p165

Poetry 2

1   Which poem by Robert Burns is traditionally recited on 25 January?
2   Name the Scottish poet who was known as 'the Ettrick Shepherd'.
3   *A Child's Garden of Verses* is an anthology of poetry for children. Who wrote it?
4   Where was the poet Iain Crichton Smith born?
5   Who wrote *Under the Eildon Tree*?
6   Who wrote *A Drunk Man Looks at the Thistle*?
7   This poet was born on the island of Raasay in 1911 and is acclaimed as one of the finest Gaelic poets of all time. What is his name?
8   Who wrote 'The Cottar's Saturday Night'?
9   Which part of Scotland did George Mackay Brown come from?
10 Which Scottish writer wrote *The Lay of the Last Minstrel*?
11 Where was the poet Allan Ramsay born?
12 Name the writer and poet who was also Sir Walter Scott's son-in-law.
13 In which year was the poet Edwin Morgan born?
14 *The Golden Treasury of Scottish Poetry* (1993 edition) was edited by which Scottish poet?
15 Which Glasgow poet wrote *The Pleasures of Hope* in 1799?
16 Which poet had a volume of poetry entitled *The Labyrinth* published in 1949?
17 This poet was also a naturalist and a clergyman, first in the Scottish church and then in the Church of England. Who was he?
18 Which poet, who died in 2006, was responsible for the garden named Little Sparta?
19 Which Scottish poet and playwright translated *Tartuffe* into Glaswegian?
20 Who wrote about Leerie the Lamplighter?
21 Who published poetry, supposedly by Ossian, in 1762-63?
22 What was the profession of poet Sorley Maclean?
23 Who wrote 'In Memoriam James Joyce'?
24 *The Queen's Wake* is a volume of poems by which poet?
25 Which Scottish poet was named as the first female Poet Laureate in 2009?

Answers: p166

Central Scotland & Tayside

1   Which river flows through Dunblane?

2   Which loch provides most of Glasgow's water?

3   Which school was founded by John McNabb?

4   Which mountain is 'the fairy mountain of the Caledonians'?

5   In which Tayside town did the dispute take place which led ultimately to the Disruption?

6   Blairgowrie is now known for the soft fruit that is grown in the region, but on what industry did the town build its wealth in the nineteenth century?

7   In which year did William Wallace take Stirling Castle?

8   Is Ben Ledi, by Callander, a Munro?

9   Which two rivers flow through Doune?

10 In which house near Fettercairn can visitors see a collection of Gladstone memorabilia?

11 What song was written by Robert Burns about the countryside around Aberfeldy?

12 Which organization manages the site of Bannockburn?

13 What is the name of the hill by Scone Palace where kings of Scotland were once crowned?

14 From which river was Loch Faskally created?

15 What tragedy is said to have struck the village of Balfron three centuries ago?

16 Where was 'Perkin's Mauve' famously used?

17 What is the highest mountain in Perthshire?

18 Which saint is believed to be buried in Balquhidder?

19 From which century does the tower of the ruined Muthill Church date?

20 In which Perthshire town can be found the Little Houses?

21 Which educational institution is situated in the Airthrey Estate?

22 Near which loch is Ardvorlich House?

23 Which architect designed Kinross House?

24 In which century was the library at Innerpeffray opened?

25 Through which hills does Gleneagles run?

Answers: p166

The Life & Career of Sean Connery

1 In which year was Sean Connery born?
2 What was the name of his father?
3 What was the maiden name of his mother?
4 What was the name Sean Connery's parents gave him?
5 Why did Sean Connery leave the navy?
6 In what year did he recieve an honorary degree from Heriot-Watt University?
7 What is the name of Sean Connery's son?
8 Who co-starred with Connery in *Family Business*?
9 In which year was *The Hill* released?
10 What is the name of Sean Connery's second wife?
11 Which film, set in the depths of the jungle, did Connery star in in 1992?
12 What role did Sean Connery play in *Robin Hood, Prince of Thieves*?
13 What is the name of Sean Connery's stepson?
14 What was the second Bond film in which Sean Connery starred?
15 When was Sean Connery made a Freeman of Edinburgh?
16 What was the name of the first film in which he appeared?
17 What sport does Sean Connery play and watch for relaxation?
18 In which year did he appear in *Dr No*?
19 What was the name of the 1965 film in which fellow Scot Ian Bannen starred with Connery?
20 Whom did Sean Connery marry in 1962?
21 What part did Sean Connery play in *The Untouchables*?
22 In which film did Connery appear as Colonel Arbuthnot?
23 What year was *Never Say Never Again* released?
24 In which film did Sean Connery co-star with Harrison Ford in 1989?
25 In what 2003 film did he star in?

Answers: p167

General Knowledge 18

1   Name two former inmates of the Special Unit at Barlinnie Prison who, while they were there, discovered they had considerable artistic ability, particularly in sculpting.

2   Who is the author of the 'Katie Morag' books?

3   What are the colours of Partick Thistle Football Club?

4   How was Skara Brae discovered?

5   Which position was taken up by Lord Gordon of Strathblane in 1998?

6   In which decade was Scottish Ballet formed?

7   What is the name of the company owned by wealthy Scottish businessman Brian Souter?

8   Which king banned golf and football in 1457?

9   What was a 'leister' and what was it used for?

10   What is the Scottish Blackface?

11   Name the Scot who made the first ascent of the southwest face of Everest.

12   What is the name of the town which features in *The House with the Green Shutters*?

13   Which two Scottish brewing firms merged in 1931 to form Scottish Brewers?

14   In which decade was the Bilingualism Project launched in some primary schools in the Outer Isles?

15   In which Scottish industry was the Egyptian water wheel once used?

16   Why was one Scottish locomotive nicknamed 'the Diver'?

17   Which Scottish footballer distinguished himself by being sent off during his first game as player/manager?

18   In which area of the world of music has Ian Hamilton made his name?

19   Who collected a *Tea-Table Miscellany*?

20   In which decade was the Scottish Law Comission established?

21   Which famous Scottish artist painted *The Vegetable Stall*?

22   Who designed the bridge at Dunkeld?

23   Where is the Phoenix 369 Gallery?

24   What relationship did James VII bear to William of Orange?

25   In which year were Glasgow and Edinburgh first linked by rail?

Answers: p167

History 2

1 Name the Liberal politician who founded the Territorial Army.
2 What was the main reason why Keir Hardie lost his parliamentary seat in 1915?
3 Name the Scottish general who handed Charles I over to parliament in 1646.
4 Who were the parents of Mary II?
5 In which year was James Maxton expelled from the House of Commons?
6 In which year was the Second Book of Discipline drawn up?
7 Agnes Sampson was tortured and put to death at North Berwick for witchcraft. What other charge was laid against her?
8 Who was consecrated Archbishop of St Andrews in 1660?
9 In whose reign did the Union of the Parliaments of Scotland and England take place?
10 When was the Glorious Revolution?
11 Who was the mother of the Old Pretender?
12 What was the last battle won by Bonnie Prince Charlie before his defeat at Culloden?
13 In which year did James VI sign the Confession of Faith?
14 When did the Gowrie Conspiracy take place?
15 In which year did the evacuation of St Kilda take place?
16 When did the pupils of Edinburgh High School riot?
17 When was the Caledonian Canal opened?
18 Who was responsible for the burning of Elgin Cathedral?
19 Which Highland town was founded in 1776?
20 In which year did the Old Pretender leave Scotland for good?
21 What were the two warring factions in the Battle of the Braes?
22 In which year did Mary, Queen of Scots, marry Bothwell?
23 In which year was Elgin Cathedral burned?
24 Where did John Balliol abdicate?
25 In which year did James IV marry?

Answers: p168

Edinburgh

1   What is the name of Edinburgh's extinct volcano?
2   In which century was the Abbey of Holyrood founded?
3   Which hotel stands at the corner of Lothian Road and Princes Street?
4   Name the street that stretches from Edinburgh Castle to Holyrood Palace.
5   Name the wall that was built to add to the city's defences in the early sixteenth century.
6   Where is the Scott Monument?
7   Who was murdered in Holyrood Palace in 1566?
8   Name the hidden street that lies below the City Chambers in Edinburgh.
9   By which signal can the citizens of Edinburgh set their clocks each day?
10 What draws hundreds of spectators to the castle esplanade in August every year?
11 Where is the Heart of Midlothian?
12 Which famous animal has a statue in his memory on the George IV Bridge?
13 From which century does Edinburgh's New Town date?
14 Which seaside resort, named after a town in Panama, was the first to have bathing machines?
15 Where was the Nor' Loch?
16 What was a 'Luckenbooth'?
17 Which two galleries stand at the foot of the Mound?
18 How frequently does the Edinburgh Book Festival take place?
19 Meadowbank Stadium was built for which games?
20 What is the name of the 'unofficial' arm of the Edinburgh Festival?
21 What is the name of the famous cannon at Edinburgh Castle?
22 Where is the Witches Well?
23 With what cry did the citizens of Edinburgh's Old Town dispose of their waste matter out of their windows at ten o'clock every night?
24 Who designed the buildings on the north side of Charlotte Square?
25 What is the name of the bridge designed by Telford that spans the Water of Leith at the west end of town?

Answers: p168

Politics 2

1 Where was Gordon Brown born?
2 Who was leader of the Labour Party from 1992 to 1994?
3 When was the Scottish Nationalist Party founded?
4 Who became first minister in November 2000?
5 When was the first seat in Westminster won by an SNP candidate?
6 Which position did Malcolm Rifkind hold in the Cabinet immediately before the general election of 1997?
7 In which industry did Keir Hardie begin his working life?
8 Who was the first Conservative woman minister?
9 Where is the site of the new Scottish Parliament Building?
10 Which prime minister was forced to resign in 1855 over the Crimean War?
11 Who became leader of the Scottish National Party in 1990?
12 How many seats did the Labour Party win in Scotland in the 1997 general election?
13 How many Scottish prime ministers of Britain have there been, including Tony Blair?
14 Whom did Tony Blair appoint as chancellor of the exchequer in 1997?
15 For how many years did Malcolm Rifkind hold the same seat in parliament?
16 In which year did Katharine, Duchess of Atholl, resign her seat in parliament?
17 Which political party does Gavin Strang represent?
18 Where are the headquarters of the Scottish National Party?
19 How many MPs does Scotland have in the House of Commons?
20 In which election was the Conservative party defeated in every constituency in Scotland?
21 In what year did Sir Henry Campbell-Bannerman become prime minister?
22 What was the name of the committed Marxist who became the first Soviet Consul in Scotland?
23 Name the socialist leader, born in Scotland of Irish parents, who was executed for his part in the Easter Rising in 1916.
24 Which Scottish literary figure became MP for the Scottish Universities in 1927?
25 Who was appointed the first president of the Scottish Labour Party in 1888?

Answers: p169

General Knowledge 19

1   Which well-known author assisted in the appeal against the conviction of Oscar Slater for murder?

2   Which song do the following lines come from?
'It's the call of sea and shore,
It's the tang of bog and peat,
And the scent of brier and myrtle
That puts magic in our feet.'

3   Name the daughter of Malcolm Canmore who married Henry I.

4   What invention by James Dewar has brought warmth to many a cold outing in Scotland and elsewhere?

5   Where did the philosopher Adam Ferguson go to university?

6   What was the middle name of Scots journalist Alastair Dunnett?

7   Which Scottish medical pioneer, knighted in 1944, won a Nobel Prize in 1945?

8   In which country did nineteenth-century industrialist James Finlayson establish the textile factory of Oy Finlayson Ab?

9   How many King Jameses died a natural death?

10 Who was the only surviving direct descendent in the House of Canmore after the death of Alexander III?

11 Name the Scottish author of *Ice Station Zebra*.

12 Through which mountain range does the Lairig Ghru run?

13 Which Scots pop group urged their fans to 'Keep on Dancin'?

14 Which football club did rock singer Jim Kerr try to buy?

15 With which two industries is the name of Sir Ian Kinloch McGregor associated?

16 Which university has taken over the former Thomas Clouston Clinic at Craiglockhart in Edinburgh?

17 With which city is architect Archibald Simpson most associated?

18 When was the Tay Road Bridge opened?

19 With which four teams did Gordon Strachan play during his professional footballing career?

20 Where in the west of Scotland was Nobel's British Dynamite Factory located?

21 Name the biologist and sociologist who wrote *The Evolution of Sex* in 1889 and *Cities in Evolution* in 1915.

22 During which period was former politician, Michael Forsyth, Secretary of State for Scotland?

23 After which Scottish botanist is *Gentiana forrestii* named?

24 With which branch of learning is the name of James Ferrier associated?

25 Who was the royal husband of the daughter of the 14th Earl of Strathmore?

Answers: p169

Scottish Towns & Villages

1 Where is the oldest university in Scotland?
2 Which island town's name means 'king's harbour'?
3 Which Highland village has a rare mineral named after it?
4 In which city was Dennis the Menace conceived?
5 What is the name of the spa town close to Balmoral?
6 Which clan has a museum in Newtonmore?
7 By which glen is the village of Fortingall?
8 By which river is the town of Crieff situated?
9 Where is the Tam o' Shanter Inn?
10 Which town is known as 'the capital of the Highlands'?
11 Which famous politician was born in Seatown of Lossiemouth?
12 Which Scottish fishing port was built on Bressay Sound?
13 A fish ladder and a festival theatre: which town?
14 What is the name of the village in Tayside familiar to Shakespeare lovers?
15 Which city was known as 'Auld Reekie'?
16 Which town in Ayrshire gets its name from the salt production industry?
17 On which firth is the village of Portknockie situated?
18 Which town stands at the southern end of the Caledonian Canal?
19 By which town, north of Aberdeen, is the Ugie Fish House situated?
20 From which seaside town can you take a boat trip round the Bass Rock?
21 In which border town is St Mungo's Well?
22 Where is the Goblin Ha'?
23 Which Highland port was the regular holiday haunt of the late Barbara Cartland?
24 Which town was formed from the villages of Inverallan and Pathfoot?
25 Name Scotland's first new town.

Answers: p170

Glasgow

1   Where is the Horse Shoe Bar?
2   When was Glasgow Cathedral consecrated?
3   In what year did fire wreak havoc in Glasgow, destroying almost one third of the town?
4   What is the motto of Glasgow?
5   Which station is the terminus for the Glasgow–Edinburgh railway?
6   Where is the Burrell Collection?
7   Where was the original Paddy's Market?
8   When was Glasgow University founded?
9   What does the name Glasgow (*glas-cau*) mean?
10 Where are Glasgow's City Chambers?
11 When was the People's Palace built?
12 Where would you see a fish, a ring, a tree, a bird and a bell?
13 What is the name of Glasgow's famous weekend market?
14 What would you find in the Kibble Palace?
15 Which company owned a particularly exotic factory building in Glasgow?
16 What is the name of the oldest house in Glasgow?
17 Where does Sir Walter Scott stand on high in the city?
18 Where can you see a penny farthing?
19 In what year did Glasgow play host to the Garden Festival?
20 What are the names of the three main docks constructed on the Clyde between 1864 and 1897?
21 Where in Glasgow is Provand's Lordship?
22 In which century was Glasgow Academy founded?
23 Where is the Fossil Grove?
24 In what year was Glasgow proclaimed European City of Culture?
25 What is the name of the theatre in Gorbals Street?

Answers: p170

Around & About in Scotland 3

1   Which suburb of Dundee was once known as 'the richest square mile in Europe'?
2   What and where is Scurdie Ness?
3   Where is the Speyside Cooperage?
4   Which island is known as 'the Jewel of the Hebrides'?
5   How many arches are there on the Dunkeld Bridge?
6   Which distillery is the oldest in Scotland?
7   Where did David I have a vision of a stag with a cross?
8   What is the name of Scotland's oldest continuously inhabited house?
9   What is the highest village in Scotland?
10 The grounds of which Scottish castle boast the world's longest herbaceous border?
11 In which BBC TV production did Ardverikie Estate feature?
12 Which abbey has been called 'the Iona of the East'?
13 Which town in Scotland was the first to use a power loom?
14 Which town is the former centre for justice and government for Fife?
15 Where is the Scottish Seabird Centre?
16 Where is the Armadillo?
17 Which town was once known as 'the Westminster of the North'?
18 Where is the Time Capsule?
19 In which direction would you have to travel to get from Glasgow to Prestwick Airport?
20 What is known by citizens of Glasgow as 'the Clockwork Orange'?
21 Where is Noss National Nature Reserve?
22 Where is the Scottish Vintage Bus Museum?
23 In which series of films were Glen Nevis and the Fort William to Mallaig railway line used as filming locations?
24 What is the name of the twelfth-century church at Leuchars in Fife?
25 What is the name of the fourteenth- to seventeenth-century residence of the Bishops of Moray?

Answers: p171

General Knowledge 20

1   Where is Dyce Airport?

2   Where is McCulloch's Tree and what is it?

3   Who sang 'I Love a Lassie'?

4   In which part of Scotland did the Levellers Revolt of 1724 take place?

5   Where was Allan Pinkerton born?

6   Which Scottish king married Euphemia Ross?

7   Where is Dunderave Castle?

8   What is the name of the freshwater herring found in the waters of Loch Lomond?

9   What treasures were found on Traprain Law in East Lothian?

10 Where would you go to visit Lady Stair's House?

11 Which Scottish publishing firm had its origins in the printing and publishing of educational and temperance texts?

12 Name the Scottish industrialist who worked for the Pennsylvania Railroad Company in the 1860s.

13 Where is the headquarters of the Scottish Forestry Commission?

14 Name the Scots poet who was made professor of English at St Andrews University in 1991.

15 Which story by Arthur Conan Doyle was the first featuring Sherlock Holmes?

16 Which team did Sir Alex Ferguson manage before he moved to Aberdeen?

17 Which famous Scottish patriot was made MP for Haddingtonshire in the 1670s?

18 What is the name of the hospital for disabled ex-servicemen in Renfrewshire?

19 Which tragedy in nineteenth-century Scotland was caused by *phytophthora infestans*?

20 What is Wemyss Ware and where was it produced?

21 In which year were the Magnox reactors at Hunterston 'A' closed down?

22 Which famous Scots musician was born in Inver?

23 Which fishing port in the north-east is known as 'the Broch'?

24 Where was explorer John Rae born?

25 Who/what was Peaty Sandy?

Answers: p171

Rivers, Lochs & Falls

1   Which two rivers flow into the sea at Aberdeen?
2   Which three lochs form part of the Caledonian Canal between Loch Linnhe and Loch Ness?
3   In which century did work first begin on the Clyde to make its waters deeper between Glasgow and Port Glasgow?
4   What is the name of the deepest loch in Scotland?
5   What is the name of the largest loch in Scotland?
6   What is the name of the sea loch which cuts into the west coast at Tarbert?
7   Which river passes through Dumfries before joining the Solway Firth?
8   Where is the source of the Water of Leith?
9   What are the names of the two lochs at either end of the Trossachs?
10 Which river joins the Forth at Cramond, in the north-west of Edinburgh?
11 Near the head of which loch is Dalwhinnie?
12 What is the highest waterfall in Britain?
13 On which loch was Mary, Queen of Scots, held against her will?
14 What is the name of the river that flows through the Pass of Killiecrankie?
15 What is the name of the river that is spanned by Rumbling Bridge?
16 Which waterfall is known as 'the Gloomy Falls'?
17 Where does the Scottish River Tyne meet the sea?
18 When was the Forth Road Bridge opened?
19 What is the name of Scotland's second longest river?
20 'And me and my true love will never meet again . . .' Where?
21 What is the name of the source of the River Tweed?
22 Where is the source of the River Clyde?
23 To the nearest five miles, how long is the River Forth?
24 What is the name of the longest river in Scotland?
25 What is the name of the biggest tributary of the River Spey?

Answers: p172

Literature 3

1   Where is Alastair MacLean's *When Eight Bells Toll* set?
2   What is the subject matter of *The Silver Bough* by F. Marian McNeill?
3   Who was the father of Naomi Mitchison?
4   Which nineteenth-century writer used the pen-name Fiona MacLeod?
5   Which historical event featured in *Consider the Lilies*?
6   Who wrote *The Adventures of an Atom*?
7   Where did Muriel Spark live for some years after she was married?
8   Which book by Robert Louis Stevenson describes his own travels in France?
9   Who wrote under the pseudonym of Christopher North?
10 Who wrote *The Lymond Saga*?
11 For whom was *The Wind in the Willows* written?
12 Who wrote *The Steps to the Empty Throne*?
13 To which group of writers did Mrs Margaret Oliphant belong?
14 Who wrote *A Life of Byron* in 1830?
15 What is the profession of the central character in *Mr Alfred MA* by George Friel?
16 What were the first names of two Scots novelists and sisters, the Findlaters?
17 Who wrote *A History of the Five Jameses* in the early seventeenth century?
18 Who wrote *The Rodney Stone*?
19 What was the name of the first novel published by J. Leslie Mitchell?
20 In which part of Scotland was contemporary Scots writer Duncan McLean born?
21 Which famous children's book begins with the words 'The Mole had been working hard all the morning, spring-cleaning his little home'?
22 What is the name of the central character in Robin Jenkins's *Happy for the Child*?
23 Which Scottish author's first book, *The Cutting Room*, won the 2002 John Creasey (New Blood) Dagger Award?
24 Which city was chosen as UNESCO City of Literature in 2004?
25 What is the name of the Glasgow book festival that takes place annually in the Mitchell Library?

Answers: p172

Whisky

1   From which century does the first written evidence of whisky distillation date?

2   In which year was the Whisky Association founded?

3   In 1942, the Whisky Association was replaced by another organization to protect the whisky trade in Scotland. What was the new organization called?

4   What is the name of the instrument which measures the proof of the spirit?

5   In which century was the patent still invented?

6   Once germination of the barley to be used has reached the right stage for the next part of the distillation process, how is the germination checked?

7   What kind of still is used to produce malt whisky?

8   Which island is particularly well known for its malt whiskies?

9   Where does Highland Park Whisky come from?

10 What is the name for the container in which the ground barley is mixed with boiling water to dissolve the starch?

11 Where is the Glenfiddich Distillery?

12 In which decade was Distillers Company Limited formed?

13 What event overseas contributed to a slump in the whisky trade in the 1920s?

14 What is a blended whisky?

15 Where is Laphroaig distilled?

16 In the pot-still distilling process, what is the name of the liquid that is drawn off after the sugar from the barley has been dissolved in it?

17 What name is associated with Red Label and Black Label?

18 Which whisky was recommended 'afore ye go'?

19 In which part of Scotland is Glenkinchie Distillery?

20 In which part of Scotland is the Macallan Distillery?

21 Can Scotch whisky be made outside Scotland?

22 When was Scottish Malt Distillers Ltd formed?

23 What were DCL's patent-still distilleries used for during the First World War?

24 In 2001, a bottle of 60-year-old malt whisky was sold at auction at McTear's in Glasgow for more than £15,000. What was the name of the whisky?

25 What was the approximate value of Scotland's whisky exports in 2008?
    a) 3 billion b) 20 million c) 1 billion

Answers: p173

General Knowledge 21

QUESTIONS

1. After the deaths of Alexander III and the Maid of Norway, who were the two main contenders for the Scottish throne?
2. How many kings of Scotland were called Malcolm?
3. Which Dundee team plays in orange strips?
4. In which part of the United States is the SS *Queen Mary* now berthed?
5. Of which river is the Beltie Burn a tributary?
6. What was the profession of Sir Arthur Conan Doyle?
7. Which football team plays at McDiarmid Park on the outskirts of Perth?
8. In which century was the Duke of Atholl granted the right to keep a 'private' army?
9. Before St Andrews Cathedral was built, what was the most important cathedral in Scotland?
10. What was the CWC, formed in 1915?
11. Name the Scot who starred in the TV series *The Man from UNCLE* and now stars in the US TV series *NCIS*.
12. To the nearest five metres, how high is the village of Tomintoul?
13. Who was the SFWA's Footballer of the Year in 1980?
14. Who founded the Society of Antiquaries of Scotland?
15. Who wrote 'Scotland the Brave'?
16. Which mountain is known as 'the Cobbler'?
17. For which occasion was the Edinburgh Tartan designed and manufactured?
18. With which town is the name of Dewar most associated?
19. What name became inextricably linked with cartography in Edinburgh?
20. Whom did Elizabeth Bowes-Lyon marry?
21. Where is Cannonball House?
22. What is the motto of Glasgow University?
23. On which island is the village of Ardminish?
24. Who provided the money to build what is now known as the Central Library in Edinburgh?
25. Where is the eastern terminal of the Forth-Clyde Canal?

Answers: p173

92

Life & Works of Robert Louis Stevenson

1   Who illustrated *A Child's Garden of Verses*?

2   Did Robert Louis Stevenson have any brothers or sisters?

3   Which book by Robert Louis Stevenson describes a journey by canoe?

4   What journey is Stevenson describing in *The Amateur Immigrant*?

5   What was the name of the historical novel for children which Stevenson wrote, published in 1888?

6   Where was Stevenson living when he wrote *The Master of Ballantrae*?

7   What did Stevenson originally go to university to study?

8   What was the second career for which Stevenson trained?

9   In which year was Robert Louis Stevenson born?

10   In which novel does Alan Breck feature?

11   With whom did Robert Louis Stevenson collaborate in playwriting?

12   What place is the subject of *Ille Terrarum*?

13   From what illness did Stevenson suffer for much of his life?

14   What ultimately caused Stevenson's death?

15   What was the name of the short story collection published in 1882?

16   In which year was *A Child's Garden of Verses* published?

17   In which year did Stevenson and his family finally settle in Samoa?

18   What was the name of the woman whom Stevenson married?

19   Who collaborated with Robert Louis Stevenson in writing *The Wrecker* and *The Wrong Box*?

20   In which century is *Kidnapped* set?

21   What was the Christian name of Robert Louis Stevenson's father?

22   What is the title of the sequel to *Kidnapped*?

23   What was the name of Stevenson's stepdaughter?

24   In which year did Robert Louis Stevenson die?

25   Name the learned friend of Stevenson's who provided him with valuable literary criticism, help and advice throughout his life.

Answers: p174

Great Scots 3

1   Name the philosopher who was Keeper of the Advocates Library in Edinburgh in the 1750s.

2   In which continent did Mungo Park meet his death?

3   Name the Scots author of *The Divided Self*.

4   Which Scottish saint is said to have founded the abbey of Durrow in Ireland?

5   Which Scottish philosopher is commemorated with a monument on Calton Hill?

6   What tree is named after David Douglas, the famous botanist?

7   Who won the Nobel Prize for Chemistry in 1957?

8   Who was sent to France to escape the dangers of 'the Rough Wooing'?

9   Which Scottish theologian was nicknamed 'the Blast'?

10 In which decade was Charles Rennie Mackintosh born?

11 Which twentieth-century minister translated the New Testament from Greek into Scots?

12 How was the 'Red Fox' killed?

13 Which great Scots mathematician was born in Merchiston Castle, Edinburgh?

14 Which Scottish engineer entered into a manufacturing business partnership with Matthew Boulton?

15 In which country did Thomas Glover make his name and his fortune?

16 Name the famous Scottish sports commentator who began his working life as a teacher of PE.

17 Name the Scottish architect who succeeded his brother Robert as Architect of the King's Works in 1769.

18 Which famous Scottish Quaker was non-resident Governor of East New Jersey in the late seventeenth century?

19 In what profession did John Smith, former leader of the Labour Party, train?

20 Which future king of Scotland went into battle against his own father?

21 In which year did Anne, daughter of James VII, become Queen of Great Britain and Ireland?

22 Who was the Scottish economist who wrote *Inquiry into the Nature and Causes of the Wealth of Nations*?

23 When was the philosopher David Hume born?

24 Who was the geologist and writer who wrote *Scenes and Legends of the North of Scotland*?

25 Which Scottish criminologist wrote accounts of the trials of William Pritchard, Madeleine Smith and Oscar Slater, among others?

Answers: p174

Battles

1. When was the Battle of Bannockburn fought?
2. Who emerged as victors in the Battle of Pinkie?
3. Who led the English troops in the Battle of Prestonpans?
4. When was the Battle of Stirling Bridge fought?
5. Who led the English troops at the Battle of Culloden?
6. What was the date of the Battle of Culloden?
7. Who led the Scottish troops in the Battle of Dunbar?
8. Which battle, fought in 1679, was a significant defeat for the Covenanters?
9. Against whom were the Covenanters victorious in the Battle of Philiphaugh in 1645?
10. At which battle did John Claverhouse lose his life?
11. Which battle was fought in 1513?
12. Where was Mary, Queen of Scots, defeated by Moray in 1568?
13. What battle was fought between the Saxons and the Picts in 1685?
14. At what battle was Malcolm III killed in 1093?
15. Who commanded the Scots at the Battle of Stirling Bridge?
16. In which battle, in 1388, did the Earl of Douglas defeat the English under the command of Henry Percy?
17. Who commanded the Jacobite forces that were defeated at the Battle of Sheriffmuir?
18. When was the Battle of Largs?
19. Which side won the Battle of Ancrum: Scots or English?
20. Which king was killed after the Battle of Sauchieburn?
21. When did the Battle of Kilsyth take place?
22. In which battle in 1679 was Viscount Dundee beaten by the Covenanters?
23. When was the Battle of Falkirk?
24. When was the Battle of Dunkeld?
25. Where was Dalyell's victory over the Covenanters in 1666?

Answers: p175

General Knowledge 22

1 Where is most of the work on the *Book of Kells* thought to have been done?
2 Which nineteenth-century judge made his home at Craigcrook Castle in Edinburgh?
3 What was the name of the Norwegian king involved in the Battle of Largs?
4 What were manufactured at Cowlairs in Springburn?
5 Which treaty secured the release of James I from captivity?
6 Which clan became known as 'the clan without a name'?
7 In which century were the counties of Ross and Cromarty amalgamated?
8 Which company built the *Discovery*?
9 Which loch is the third longest in Scotland?
10 'Round and round the radical road, the radical rascal ran . . .' Where is the radical road?
11 In which decade was the land for the present Hampden Park Stadium acquired?
12 How many Orkney islands are there?
    a) 36 b) 75 c) 67
13 Which industry was associated with the River North Esk and Penicuik until the 1970s?
14 With what kind of business is the name of Daniel Macmillan associated?
15 Which town was nicknamed 'the Charing Cross of the Highlands'?
16 Where is the St Fergus Gas Terminal?
17 What was the name of Rob Roy MacGregor's wife?
18 Where is the Forge Shopping Centre?
19 What is the name of the important archaeological site on Mainland Shetland, near Sumburgh?
20 When did the Pentland Rising take place?
21 Which prominent thinker was elected Lord Rector of Edinburgh University in 1866?
22 In which decade did the Eyemouth fishing disaster take place?
23 By what name is *colicoides impunctatus*, scourge of the Highland summer, more commonly known?
24 In which two branches of the services did the author known as Lewis Grassic Gibbon serve?
25 How many items are in the Scottish Regalia?

Answers: p175

Aberdeenshire, Moray & Highland

1 In which museum in Fort William is there 'a secret portrait' of Bonnie Prince Charlie?

2 How many locks are there in Neptune's Staircase?

3 Where is St Conan's Kirk?

4 Where are the remains of Rob Roy MacGregor buried?

5 Which loch is crossed by the Corran Ferry?

6 Which town was demolished and rebuilt to make way for a castle?

7 Name the famous Scottish fiddler/composer who was born in Banchory.

8 Where is the seat of the Duke of Sutherland?

9 On which loch is the town of Lairg situated?

10 What drew people to Strathpeffer in Victorian times?

11 On the outskirts of which town is the Glengarioch Distillery?

12 On which loch is Castle Tioram situated?

13 Where is the terminus of the West Highland Railway?

14 Where does the Caledonian Canal join Loch Ness?

15 Where is the start of the Devil's Staircase?

16 Where is Cape Oreas, referrered to by Greek historian, Diodorus Siculus, in his writing?

17 Which Highland town, site of a major distillery, was once also a centre of the aluminium industry?

18 What is the name of the nature reserve that is situated to the south-east of Loch Maree?

19 What is the name of the man who established the gardens at Inverewe?

20 What is the name of the Benedictine abbey situated a few miles to the south-west of Elgin?

21 In which century was the town of Grantown-on-Spey founded?

22 Which castle in Aberdeenshire has towers called Preston, Meldrum, Seton, Gordon and Leith?

23 After which king is Fort William so called?

24 Where was the Brahan Seer put to death?

25 In which loch is Macphee's Island?

Answers: p176

Perth

1   Where did John Knox preach in 1559?
2   Who was 'the Fair Maid of Perth'?
3   What is the name of the oldest established hotel in Scotland?
4   Where is the Regimental Headquarters and Museum of the Black Watch?
5   Which famous figure was moved from the High Street to King Street?
6   Who owns the Branklyn Garden?
7   Which Perth family's business interests moved from umbrellas to dye to dry cleaning?
8   When was the worst recorded flood in the history of Perth?
9   Who moved from Muirton Park to the Crieff Road?
10 When was the Fergusson Gallery opened?
11 What was swept away in the flood of 1621?
12 Which building makes a connection between whisky and curling?
13 Where will you find Ave Maria, Johannes Baptiste and Agnus Dei?
14 In which century was the King James VI Golf Club founded?
15 In which year were the four monasteries around Perth devastated by Reformers?
16 When was the Perth Civic Trust founded?
17 What event took place on the North Inch in 1397?
18 Who designed Perth Bridge?
19 How many bells are there in St John's Kirk?
20 When was Perth City Hall built?
21 Which two men were responsible for the land purchase, plans and building of Perth's New Town in the eighteenth century?
22 Where is the Perth Museum and Art Gallery?
23 In which year were three women put to death for witchcraft on the North Inch?
24 Where was Little Willie found?
25 Where did Arthur Bell begin his career in whisky blending and retailing?

Answers: p176

Mary, Queen of Scots

1 In which year did the Babington Conspiracy take place?
2 How many men altogether acted as regent in the troubled period after Mary's abdication?
3 Who was the first regent after Mary's abdication?
4 Who held out Edinburgh Castle for Mary following her imprisonment?
5 What relationship did Mary bear to Henry VII of England?
6 What were the surnames of 'the Four Marys'?
7 Whom did Mary declare an outlaw within a week of her wedding to Darnley?
8 Who was presiding clergyman at the infant James's baptism?
9 In which church did Mary marry the Dauphin of France?
10 In which year did the Dauphin die?
11 In which year was the child Mary sent to France?
12 What two titles were conferred upon Lord Darnley by Mary, just before his marriage to her?
13 Where did Darnley fall ill?
14 What title was given to Bothwell by Mary just before he married her?
15 Who owned the castle at Loch Leven where Mary was kept prisoner?
16 What was the name of Bothwell's first wife?
17 Before he married Mary, Bothwell had to obtain an annulment of his first marriage. Who granted the annulment?
18 Who was the last regent before King James VI assumed power?
19 Where did Bothwell and Mary see each other for the last time?
20 Where was Mary taken immediately after her surrender at Carberry?
21 Where were Mary's forces defeated after her escape from Loch Leven Castle?
22 What happened to Archbishop Hamilton after Dumbarton Castle was taken?
23 When was Regent Moray assassinated?
24 When was the Pacification of Perth?
25 Who followed Moray as regent?

Answers: p177

General Knowledge 23

1 Where is the Royal Dick School of Veterinary Studies?
2 Which English poet was mistakenly arrested as a spy at Fort Augustus during a visit to Scotland?
3 In which country did explorer Hugh Clapperton die?
4 What sport were 'crampits' once used for?
5 Which two saints are said to have met at the Molendinar Burn?
6 Around which industry did the town of Lerwick grow up?
7 In which part of Scotland is Loch Quoich?
8 Who was Scottish philosopher James Mill's famous son?
9 Name the eminent politician who was born in Holytown in 1856.
10 What are Scotland's two native conifers?
11 On which of the Flannan Isles is St Flannan's Chapel?
12 Who was defeated at the Battle of Dalry?
13 In which decade was the Gaelic Books Council set up?
14 Who donated money to Iona to establish a library?
15 In which century was the first National Mod held?
16 What was the name of Harry Lauder's wife?
17 Where is the island of Inchkenneth?
18 In which century was the Scottish Grand Lodge of Freemasons formed?
19 What was the name of Charles I's older brother?
20 Which port near Edinburgh is a centre for chemical refining?
21 Where is Kinnoull Hill?
22 Where was the first teacher training institution in Scotland (and Britain)?
23 In which century was the Monkland Canal opened?
24 In which of Scotland's new towns will you find the Kingdom Shopping Centre?
25 Who lived at 9 Brechin Road, Kirriemuir?

Answers: p177

Inverness

1. What was the name of the radio station based in Inverness?
2. Which English writer described Inverness as 'the capital of the Highlands'?
3. Which building is the oldest in the city?
4. What is the name of the cathedral in Inverness?
5. In which century was the cathedral built?
6. During the reign of which king did Inverness become a royal burgh?
7. What is the name of Inverness's theatre?
8. In which century did the railway reach Inverness?
9. Whose troops attacked Inverness in 1645?
10. What is the name of the airport for Inverness?
11. Where is the Museum and Art Gallery?
12. What is the *Clach-na-Cudainn*?
13. From which century does the present castle date?
14. What is the name of the fifth-century BC hill-fort by Inverness?
15. Which architect designed the cathedral?
16. From which century does Dunbar's Hospital date?
17. Which order of monks once had a monastery in the town?
18. In which street is the Mercat Cross?
19. From which century does Abertarff House date?
20. Where is the High Church situated?
21. From which century does the old Court House date?
22. Where in Inverness did Lloyd George and Winston Churchill meet in 1921?
23. What is the name of the Bronze Age burial site close to the city?
24. Near which battle site is the Bronze Age burial site to be found?
25. In which decade was the seventeenth-century stone bridge over the River Ness destroyed by flood?

Answers: p178

The Romans in Scotland

1   Where was an exciting Roman find made in 1998 by a ferryman?
2   Which two rivers were connected by the Antonine Wall?
3   In which century was the Antonine Wall built?
4   What is the name of the Roman road that was built between Jedburgh and Dalkeith?
5   What was the Roman name for the fort now known as Newstead?
6   When did the Romans first invade the north of Scotland?
7   How many forts were built along the route of the Antonine Wall?
8   Where was the fort of Inchtuthil built?
9   Who led the Romans in the Battle of Mons Graupius?
10 What was the Roman name for Scotland?
11 Which Roman emperor came to Britain in AD 208 to try to quell the troublesome people from the north?
12 Which Roman general was put in charge of the construction of the Antonine Wall?
13 In which part of Scotland is the Roman fortress of Auchinhove?
14 Where was the Roman fortress that was built near Dunblane?
15 When did Agricola return to Rome from Scotland?
16 Where was the only Roman milestone in Scotland found?
17 Before the Antonine Wall was built, what construction marked the northern boundary of the Roman Empire, keeping out the marauding northern tribes?
18 Where can most of the relics from the fort at Newstead be seen?
19 When did the Romans return to the fort at Newstead after abandoning it around AD 100?
20 Which Roman historian wrote an account of the life of Agricola, giving us an insight into the first attempts to conquer Scotland?
21 In what year did the Battle of Mons Graupius take place?
22 Where is the Roman fort of Rough Castle?
23 Which modern road follows the track of Dere Street?
24 Which Roman emperor ordered the first invasion of Scotland?
25 Who was the last Roman emperor to try to subdue the people of Scotland?

Answers: p178

Heroes & Villains 1

1   Which Scot was responsible for founding America's national parks?

2   In which year was William Wallace executed?

3   Where did 'Black Agnes' fight off the English?

4   How did 'Bluidy Clavers' meet his death?

5   Name the Scottish founder of the SAS.

6   How and where did William Kidd die?

7   Who founded the Ragged Schools?

8   Name the Scots born mass-murderer whose crimes were discovered when the bodies of his victims blocked the drains of his London home.

9   Which football manager became the President of Manchester United Football Club in 1980?

10   Name the head of a family of cannibals who terrorized south-west Scotland for many years in the seventeenth century.

11   What is the name of the Scottish industrialist who founded the mill-town at New Lanark?

12   Which Scots hero was excommunicated in 1306?

13   Who was 'the Wizard of the West Bow'?

14   What was William Quarrier's outstanding achievement?

15   Name the serial murderer hanged in Glasgow in 1958.

16   Name the Edinburgh surgeon who was supplied with bodies by Burke and Hare.

17   Which Scots woman, accused of murdering her sweetheart, caused scandal when her letters were read out in court?

18   An extremely learned man of the thirteenth century, his name came to be associated not only with scholarly pursuits but also with wizardry. He is believed to be buried in Melrose Abbey. Some say he haunts there. Who was he?

19   Who was the Scottish miner who founded the Scottish Labour Party?

20   How did Dr Pritchard kill his wife and his mother-in-law?

21   Which city did the courageous missionary, Mary Slessor, come from?

22   Name the Olympic athlete and missionary who refused to run on the Sabbath.

23   Hopes were pinned on this man to become the Labour prime minister of Great Britain, but he died suddenly in 1994. What was his name?

24   What was the name of the laird of Buckholme Tower who slaughtered two Covenanters awaiting trial in the cellars of his home?

25   Name the Scots woman who took ambulances and medical help to troops in Serbia in the First World War.

Answers: 179

1 Where are the Rozelle House Galleries?

2 Where is Fife Airport?

3 With which group of artists is the name of Sir John Lavery associated?

4 In which century was the Children's Village of Humbie founded?

5 Where was the wedding of Stella McCartney and Alasdhair Willis held in August 2003?

6 In which year was Torness Power Station completed?

7 From which Scottish port did the Darien Expedition set sail?

8 Where are the headquarters of the SCWS?

9 What was the main cargo of the *Cutty Sark*?

10 In which decade was the recipe for the drink which was to become known as Irn-Bru first developed?

11 Which agency is responsible for the upkeep of Edinburgh Castle?

12 In which city is the Fountain Brewery?

13 Which pipe band played at Stella McCartney's wedding?

14 Which kind of monks lived at Jedburgh Abbey?

15 From which century does St Machar date?

16 From which part of Scotland did Covenanter Alexander Peden come?

17 Who designed the steamship *Rob Roy*?

18 Which town near Elie has the motto 'Mare Vivimus'?

19 How many islands are in the St Kilda group?

20 Which order of monks live in the community at Pluscarden Abbey?

21 Who was the last monarch to be born in Scotland?

22 Where is the School of Textiles and Design, formerly the Scottish College of Textiles?

23 Which body owns the site of the battlefield of Culloden?

24 Which king built the Palace at Stirling Castle?

25 What is the name of Scotland's first national park which became fully operational in 2002?

Answers: p179

Stirling

1 Who convened a parliament in Cambuskenneth Abbey in 1326?
2 With which Scots leader is Stirling Bridge associated?
3 What is sited on the Abbey Craig?
4 Where was Prince Henry, son of James VI, christened in 1594?
5 In which year was Stirling University founded?
6 In which decade was St Ninian's Church built?
7 From which century does Stirling Old Bridge date?
8 Where is Mar's Wark?
9 Who designed the Tolbooth?
10 Where is the Mercat Cross?
11 What is 'the puggy'?
12 Who commissioned the building of Argyll's Lodging?
13 Where is the Beheading Stone?
14 Which entertainment venue in the burgh was built in the seventeenth century as a charitable institution for merchants fallen on hard times?
15 Who was crowned at the Church of the Holy Rude in 1567?
16 From which century does Logie Old Kirk date?
17 What is Erskine Marykirk now used as?
18 Which Stewart monarch is buried with his wife at Cambuskenneth Abbey?
19 What is the oldest surviving part of Cambuskenneth Abbey?
20 Where Is the Ladies' Rock?
21 In which century was the town wall built?
22 From which century has the site of Stirling Castle been fortified in some way?
23 Which building in the town was funded by a legacy from Thomas Stuart Smith?
24 What famous landmark can be found in Albert Place?
25 Where is Bruce of Auchenbowie's House?

Answers: p180

History 3

1   Which Scottish king outlawed Clan Gregor and forfeited their lands?
2   In order to finance which enterprise was the Company of Scotland formed in the late seventeenth century?
3   In which year was William Wallace captured and executed?
4   In which year did the SS *Politician* sink?
5   In which year did Clydebank suffer devastation from German bombers?
6   Which Scottish explorer discovered the source of the Niger?
7   What disease caused panic in the city of Aberdeen in 1964?
8   Where was 'the Battle of the Braes' fought in 1882?
9   When did the Raid of Ruthven take place?
10 When did the last coronation take place at Scone?
11 Which Scottish king was known as 'the Red Crow'?
12 In which year did George IV make a state visit to Scotland?
13 Where was Charles I crowned?
14 When was the first Bishop's War?
15 Who led the massacre of Glencoe?
16 In which year was Robert the Bruce excommunicated?
17 Who led the troops which defeated Montrose at the Battle of Philiphaugh?
18 Who was known as 'the Red Duchess'?
19 When was the Treaty of Berwick signed?
20 In which year was the Disarming Act of 1746 repealed?
21 In which year was the medical school at Edinburgh University established?
    a) 1657 b) 1746 c) 1729
22 Through which parent could Robert the Bruce claim royal descent?
23 What sort of object is the Monymusk Reliquary?
24 In which year did the *Piper Alpha* disaster take place?
25 Which Scottish city was the most frequently bombed during the Second World War?

Answers: p180

Around & About in Scotland 4

1 Where is St Margaret's Cave?

2 Where can you visit the Tall Ship *Glenlee*?

3 What kind of artwork can be seen at the Wemyss Caves?

4 What do Benromach, Edradour and Caol Ila have in common?

5 Where do the Earl and Countess of Mansfield live?

6 Where is Scotland's first island passenger railway?

7 What is the name of the woman, burnt at the stake in 1657, whose memorial can be found at Dunning?

8 Put the following places in order, west to east: Portknockie, Buckie, Findochty.

9 What does the Star Pyramid in Stirling commemorate?

10 Where can you visit Polarama?

11 What is the name of the nineteenth-century meal mill near Carnoustie?

12 What is the longest Angus glen?

13 What is the name of the only whisky distillery pioneered by a woman?

14 What was previously known as Strathearn Hydropathic?

15 Is St Cyrus to the south or to the north of Stonehaven?

16 Where is the Loch Fad Fishery?

17 What are 'the Bullers of Buchan'?

18 In which film did Dunottar Castle feature?

19 In which village did Rudolf Hess land when he came to Scotland in 1941?

20 Which motorway connects Edinburgh and Linlithgow?

21 In which century was Stobo Castle built?

22 Where is the Eduardo Paolozzi collection housed?

23 From which century does the Round Tower in Brechin date?

24 Whose statue stands outside the Bannockburn Heritage Centre?

25 Who donated the Camera Obscura on Kirrie Hill to the town of Kirriemuir?

QUESTIONS

Answers: p181

General Knowledge 25

QUESTIONS

1   What was known as 'crotal' and what was it used for?
2   Which kind of bird was re-introduced to Scotland in 1975?
3   Where is the Brent Oil Field?
4   What is a clachan?
5   What colour are Ayrshire cattle?
6   What is the main food of the osprey?
7   Which novel by Robert Louis Stevenson was set in the village of Borgue?
8   Which famous man was drowned off the coast of Orkney in June 1916 when the HMS *Hampshire* was sunk by a mine?
9   A town in the west of Scotland, an industrial centre on North Island, New Zealand, and the capital of Bermuda all share the same name. What is it?
10 Which is the longest sea loch in Scotland?
11 Who was Queen Victoria's 'beloved friend'?
12 Where in Scotland in 1994 did a Chinook helicopter crash, killing all crew and passengers?
13 Name the theatre producer whose Highland retreat on the Nevis Estate was gutted by fire in November 2000.
14 Which body owns Brodick Castle?
15 What was the name of the minister who wrote *The Secret Commonwealth of Fairies*?
16 In which year did Ken Buchanan become flyweight champion of the world?
17 What was the former name of Glasgow Airport?
18 How many Paps of Jura are there?
19 What was the name of Rob Roy MacGregor's outlaw son, executed in 1754?
20 Which bedtime drink manufacturer once owned Gigha?
21 Which family produced a king of Scotland and (his brother) a king of Ireland within a period of ten years?
22 Which comic strip hero first appeared in the *Sunday Post* in 1936?
23 Which Scottish premier football club was Martin O'Neill associated with from 2000 to 2005?
24 What is the name of the preparatory school for Gordonstoun?
25 From whom did David Dale purchase the land for his mill town at New Lanark?

Answers: p181

Scottish Regiments

1   From which two regiments was the regiment of the Queen's Own Highlanders formed?

2   What is the tartan worn by the Scots Guards?

3   Which regimental pipe band had a number-one hit with 'Amazing Grace'?

4   What is the name of the oldest surviving Highland regiment?

5   In what year did the Cameronians disband?

6   The Royal Highland Fusiliers and The Highland Light Infantry were amalgamated in 1959. What did they become?

7   Where is the regimental museum of the Royal Scots?

8   Which regiment had its origins in the Edinburgh Regiment, raised in 1689 to defend the capital?

9   With which part of Scotland are the Gordon Highlanders associated?

10 What is the other name for the Black Watch tartan?

11 In which year were the Gordon Highlanders raised?

12 Which regiment had the motto 'Cuidich 'n Righ'?

13 With which regiment did the Royal Scots Greys amalgamate to become the Royal Scots Dragoon Guards?

14 Where is the regimental museum of the Queen's Own Highlanders?

15 Which regiment was affiliated with the 10th Princess Mary's Own Gurkha Rifles?

16 Which regiment had 'The Campbells Are Coming' as a regimental march?

17 Which regiment had Edinburgh Castle on its badge?

18 For what purpose were the companies raised that were ultimately to become the Black Watch?

19 Which tartans are worn by the men of the Argyll and Sutherland Highlanders?

20 Which regiment was sometimes referred to as 'the Greys'?

21 When did Scotland's new super-regiment, the Royal Regiment of Scotland, come into being?

22 Who raised the Scots Greys in 1681?

23 Where is the museum of the Black Watch regiment?

24 Where is the museum of the Cameronians Scottish Rifles?

25 Which Scottish regiment carried out guard duties at Buckingham Palace?

Answers: p182

Football 2

1 Who was manager of Rangers from 1978 to 1983?

2 How many times was Bill Shankly capped as a player for Scotland?

3 What is the name of the Scot who became head of the English Football Association in 1999?

4 In which year did Jock Stein leave Celtic?

5 Which team won the 1982 Scottish Cup?

6 How many goals did Scotland score in the 1986 World Cup finals?

7 In which year did Gordon Strachan win his first Scottish cap?

8 With which two English teams did Matt Busby play?

9 In which year did Gordon Strachan take over as manager of Celtic?

10 Name the hero of Scottish football who was born in Burnbank, Lanarkshire in 1922.

11 In which year did Scotland first appear in the World Cup finals?

12 Who was manager of Scotland in the 1974 World Cup?

13 Where is the home town of Caledonian Thistle?

14 When was the Scottish Women's Football Association founded?

15 Which Dundee team plays in blue and white?

16 In which year did Graeme Souness take over from Kenny Dalglish as manager at Newcastle?

17 Name the football club where Alex Ferguson began his career as a player.

18 In which year was the Scottish Premier Division formed?

19 Where is the new St Mirren Park?

20 What was the score in the Scotland v. Peru game in the 1978 World Cup?

21 In which year did Walter Smith become manager of the Scottish national team?

22 In which year did Arbroath notch up their record score of 360 against Bon Accord in the Scottish Cup?

23 During which decade was Billy Bremner a captain of Scotland?

24 Where is Ross County FC based?

25 What was the first Scottish (and British) team to compete in the European Cup?

Answers: p182

West & Central Scotland

1 On which peninsula is the town of Dunoon situated?
2 What is the Greenock Cut?
3 What are the names of the two sets of falls in the Falls of Clyde Nature Reserve?
4 By which name is Ben Arthur also known?
5 Where are the King's Caves?
6 What is the name of the port on Loch Gilp, at the entrance of the Crinan Canal?
7 Which village on Loch Lomond has been called the prettiest in Scotland?
8 Name the famous botanic garden which is situated on the Cowal Peninsula.
9 What is the name of the naval base which is situated near Garelochhead?
10 Where are 'St Columba's Footsteps'?
11 In which coastal resort of Strathclyde was John Loudon McAdam born?
12 In which town in South Lanarkshire is Scotland's only permanent puppet theatre?
13 In which part of Argyll have beavers been released in a five-year trial reintroduction?
14 Where is the Necropolis?
15 Where is the only surviving coal-fired gasworks in Scotland?
16 Where is William Wallace believed to have been born?
17 What is 'the Lang Whang'?
18 In which century was the Battle of Bothwell Brig fought?
19 On which island does the town of Millport stand?
20 Which two Scottish kings died in Dundonald Castle?
21 Where is the oldest subscription library in Scotland?
22 In which town was a famous edition of the poetry of Burns printed?
23 Which three rivers meet at Irvine?
24 Which town in Ayrshire was once famous for the manufacture of snuff boxes?
25 Where were Quarrier's Homes built?

Answers: p183

General Knowledge 26

1 Name the Scot who founded the Peninsular and Oriental Steam Navigation Company (P&O).

2 Where is the venue for the Scottish Grand National?

3 On which day of which month does the Glasgow Fair traditionally begin?

4 The car ferry *Princess Victoria* sank in 1953. Which route was she travelling?

5 Which king brought the Stone of Destiny to Scone?

6 Near which town are the ruins of Cadzow Castle?

7 What was the name of the mother of John Balliol?

8 What is the name of the comic artist who was responsible for creating the *Oor Wullie* and *The Broons* comic strips?

9 What statue stands on Haeval, overlooking Castlebay on Barra?

10 Which town on the east coast of Scotland has the motto 'Mare Ditat Rosa Decorat'?

11 What was the Bass Rock used as in the seventeenth century?

12 What is the largest National Nature Reserve in Great Britain?

13 In which year did the Bloody Friday Riot take place in Glasgow?

14 In which year were Aberdeen and London linked by rail?

15 On which island can the Kildalton Cross be found?

16 Which eighteenth-century sailor was awarded the Orders of St Vladimir and St Andrew by Catherine the Great?

17 In which decade did the Royal Botanic Garden in Edinburgh move to its present site?

18 What was the name of the woman who was the inspiration for the bride in *The Bride of Lammermoor*?

19 In which year was the King James version of the Bible published?

20 Which town changed hands between Scotland and England more than ten times in three centuries?

21 What is the brand name of North Highlands Products Ltd, a company formed by Caithness farmers as a result of an initiative launched by His Royal Highness Prince Charles to promote the economic development of the North Highlands?

22 When did Scotland's smoking ban come into force?

23 What is the full name of Bo'ness?

24 To the nearest ten miles, how long is the Antonine Wall?

25 What Scottish product was advertised as 'made in Scotland from girders'?

Answers: p183

Literature 4

1 Who wrote *Katie Stewart* in 1853?

2 What was Robert Ballantyne's most famous children's book?

3 In which city was novelist Nigel Tranter born?

4 Who wrote *Moral Fables* in the sixteenth century?

5 In which decade did Robert Ballantyne write *Martin Rattler*?

6 Where is the home town of fiction's Inspector Rebus?

7 Who was the hero of *The Thirty-Nine Steps*?

8 Who wrote a book of short stories entitled *The Acid House*?

9 Which Scottish author won the James Tait Black Memorial Prize for *Highland River*, in 1937?

10 Who wrote *The Stickit Minister*?

11 Who wrote *The House of Elrig*?

12 Which work by A.J. Cronin criticized the practices of doctors in Harley Street?

13 What was the title of Robert Garioch's account of his experiences in POW camps in the Second World War?

14 Which book by a Scottish writer features Jim Hawkins?

15 Who wrote *Janine*?

16 Name the writer of *Sartor Resartus*.

17 Where was Scots writer and journalist Allan Massie born?

18 Who wrote an autobiographical work entitled *The Company I've Kept*?

19 Who was the author of *Gallipoli Memories*?

20 Which contemporary writer is author of *The Lights Below*?

21 What is the title of Louise Welsh's first award-winning novel?

22 In which year did Iain Banks publish *A Song of Stone*?

23 Which Scottish writer and statesman was MP for the Scottish Universities from 1927 to 1935?

24 Who wrote *Just Duffy*?

25 Name the author of *Gillespie*.

Answers: p184

Great Scots 4

1   Which Scottish intellect of the nineteenth century married Jane Baillie Welsh?

2   Which historian wrote *De origine, moribus, et rebus gestis Scotorum*?

3   What was the name of the sixteenth-century prodigy, dubbed 'admirable', whose life was cut short when he was stabbed by his pupil?

4   What was the name of the man who wrote *The Handy Book of Meteorology*?

5   What was the name of the Scottish anthropologist who wrote *The Golden Bough: A Study in Comparative Religion*?

6   Which Scottish scholar, astronomer and occultist was made court astrologer by Frederick the Great?

7   What was the name of the publication which Francis, Lord Jeffrey, co-founded?

8   At which European university was theologian, Andrew Melville, a professor before he became principal at Glasgow University in 1574?

9   The subtitle of the work is 'An Attempt to Introduce the Experimental Method of Reasoning into Moral Subjects'. What is the title of the work and who wrote it?

10 Which eminent scholar, teacher and theologian was made Moderator of the General Assembly in 1567?

11 What was the name of the first Astronomer Royal for Scotland?

12 Which branch of science is generally regarded as having been founded by James Hutton?

13 Which Scottish king, a great intellectual himself, founded the University of Aberdeen?

14 What is the name of the eighteenth-century philosopher, professor of philosphy at Edinburgh for several years, who wrote *The History of the Progress and Termination of the Roman Republic*?

15 John Anderson, who died in 1796, made provision in his will for the founding of which educational institution?

16 What was the name of the founder of the 'Madras system' of education?

17 On which Scottish island was Lachlan Macquarie born?

18 With which city is the name of William Elphinstone associated?

19 Name the Scottish minister's wife and writer who published *Essays on the Superstitions of the Highlands* in the early ninenteenth century.

20 Why was 'the Wolf of Badenoch' excommunicated?

21 Which famous Scottish writer of a children's classic worked for the Bank of England in the early years of the twentieth century?

22 Which well-known Scottish legal figure had his home at Craigcrook Castle in Edinburgh?

23 Who was declared King Henry of Scotland although never crowned?

24 Which famous Scottish writer wrote in 'synthetic Scots'?

25 Who was the leader of the 'Common Sense' school of Scottish philosophers?

Plays & Theatres

1. Who wrote the play *Mary Queen of Scots Got Her Head Chopped Off*?
2. Which theatre company toured with *The Cheviot, the Stag and the Black, Black Oil*?
3. Where is the Byre Theatre?
4. Which Scottish actor is considered by some to be the embodiment of Robert Burns?
5. Where does Scotland's largest repertory company have its base?
6. Where is the Citizen's Theatre?
7. What was the real name of music-hall star Harry Lauder?
8. What is the name of the largest theatre in Aberdeen?
9. Who wrote *Ane Satyre of the Three Estaitis*?
10. Who were Francie and Josie?
11. Name the stage and television actor who married actress Una MacLean.
12. Who wrote *The Sash*?
13. In which town is the MacRobert Arts Centre?
14. Who wrote *The Gentle Shepherd*?
15. Who wrote *The Steamie*?
16. What is the name of the smallest theatre in Scotland?
17. Who wrote the *The Slab Boys* whose original cast included Robbie Coltrane?
18. Which Scottish music-hall performer is remembered for the song 'I Belong to Glasgow'?
19. Who wrote *The Hard Man* and *Animals*?
20. Where is the Traverse Theatre?
21. Which Scottish actor and comedian starred in a Scottish translation of *Le Bourgeois Gentilhomme*?
22. Where was Scots stage and film star Alastair Sim born?
23. What was the name of the theatre company set up by Robert Carlyle and four other actors in 1991?
24. Name the Scots choreographer of the Royal Ballet who died in 1992.
25. Who wrote *The Wallace*?

Answers: p185

1   Name the Scot who developed the Visible Speech System. Whose father was he?

2   Which Robert Louis Stevenson character was kidnapped and taken on board the brig *Covenant*?

3   Which sculptor was the creator of the *Big Heids* on the M8?

4   In which year was Tam Dalyell first elected to parliament?

5   Who founded the Botanic Garden in Aberdeen?

6   What is the name of Scotland's tallest tower house?

7   For what is Sir John Sholto Douglas, 8th Marquis of Queensberry, remembered?

8   From which wood are shinty sticks traditionally made?

9   In which decade was Prestwick Airport opened?

10   What were made at the Hydepark, Atlas and Queen's Park Works?

11   What is the name of the oldest house in Alloway?

12   Where is Alexander II buried?

13   Which Scottish honour was given to Princess Anne on her fiftieth birthday by the Queen?

14   What is the name of the new Scottish super-regiment?

15   What is the name of the highest mountain in Scotland?

16   Which Scottish king married Anne of Denmark?

17   At what weight did Jackie Paterson win his boxing world title in 1943?

18   In which year did Scots actor Ian Bannen die?

19   Where was singer Annie Lennox born?

20   Which Edinburgh character inspired *The Strange Case of Dr Jekyll and Mr Hyde*?

21   What was the name of the rock band formed by Alan Gordy?

22   With which Scottish stone is Queen Victoria's Mausoleum built?

23   What noble title belongs to Johnny Dumfries, the former racing driver?

24   What is the name of the Scot who founded Community Service Volunteers?

25   Which city has the busiest heliport in Scotland?

Answers: p185

Clans

1   From which common ancestor are the MacNeills of Barra and the MacNeills of Gigha thought to have been descended?

2   What does the name 'Macpherson' mean?

3   What part of Scotland does the Gordon clan originally come from?

4   Where is the home of the chief of the MacLeod clan?

5   'Cruachan!' is the slogan, or battle-cry, for which clan?

6   Eilean Donan Castle was the stronghold of which clan?

7   Which Campbell was responsible for the massacre at Glencoe?

8   Which clan chiefs were Lords of the Isles before the Stewarts took the title?

9   'Stand Fast Craigellachie' is the motto of which clan?

10 Which clan was a confederation of clans including Mackintosh, Farquharson, Macpherson, Macintyre and Cattanach among others?

11 Where did the Forbes clan have its origins?

12 What does 'Mackenzie' mean?

13 The battle-cry of the clan MacDougall is 'Buaidh no bas!' What does it mean?

14 Which clan is descended from Conn of the Hundred Battles?

15 Which part of Scotland does the MacDuff clan come from?

16 The motto of the clan MacGregor is 'Is Rioghail mo dhream'. What does it mean?

17 In which area of Scotland does the Scott clan have its origins?

18 Complete the following appellation: 'The Haughty . . .'

19 'Duke o' . . . king in Man,
    An' greatest man in a' Scotlan'.'
    What is the missing name?

20 Which clan had ivy as its clan badge?

21 From which king are the MacGregors descended?

22 In which century did the last of the MacCrimmonds die out?

23 To which clan did the Gentle Lochiel belong?

24 Robertson is a family name of which clan?

25 Of which clan was Somerled of the Isles an ancestor?

Answers: p186

Medicine in Scotland

1   Name the Scot who discovered penicillin.

2   Who was the founder of the Royal Infirmary of Edinburgh?

3   Who were the brothers from Glasgow who became eminent surgeons in the eighteenth century?

4   In which branch of medicine did James Young Simpson specialize?

5   Which university in Scotland was the first to have a chair in medicine?

6   Who identified the bacterium which causes brucellosis?

7   Who discovered a vaccine for typhoid?

8   Who, along with Sir Ronald Ross, pioneered research into malaria and discovered the connection between the mosquito and the malaria parasite?

9   Which city was the first to have an X-ray unit in a hospital?

10 In what year was the first operation performed under antiseptic conditions in Scotland by Joseph Lister?

11 Name the Scot who, along with Sir Frederick Banting and Charles Best, discovered insulin.

12 Name the electrical engineer who was one of the first to research the potential applications of radiography in medicine.

13 With which branch of medicine is the name of David Ferrier associated?

14 In what sphere of orthopaedic work was Sir William MacEwen a pioneer?

15 With which branch of medicine is the name of Andrew Duncan associated?

16 Which Scottish town was the first to introduce a special training scheme for psychiatric nurses?

17 What kind of hospital was Rottenrow?

18 Name the maternity hospital founded in Edinburgh, now closed, that was originally staffed entirely by women.

19 Name a former Edinburgh hospital in the south side of the city specializing in the treatment of women.

20 Which naval doctor wrote *A Treatise of the Scurvy* in 1753?

21 In which decade did Miranda/James Barry die?

22 Nora Wattie worked tirelessly as a pioneer of medical and social welfare in Glasgow. In which decade did she die?

23 Which prominent Scots obstetrician, Professor of Midwifery in Aberdeen from 1937 to 1965, was a campaigner for family planning and for reform of the Abortion Act?

24 What was the name of the surgeon who was the first to perform an operation in public with the use of general anaesthesia?

25 Who was the first practising doctor to be made a baronet?

Answers: p186

Food & Drink 2

1   What is the Selkirk Grace?
2   What is a girdle cake?
3   What colour is a finnan haddie?
4   For which food crop is the region around Blairgowrie best known?
5   What are the three main ingredients of shortbread?
6   What kind of fruit is a tayberry?
7   What is the main ingredient in a mealie puddin'?
8   What was 'gradan meal'?
9   What was a 'bannock stone'?
10 What was once known as a 'Crail capon'?
11 Which Scottish chef has a cook school in Port of Menteith?
12 Which foods are associated with Loch Fyne?
13 What is a Hawick Ball?
14 What is the 'other national drink' of the Scots?
15 Which international culinary award were Betty Allen and Hilary Brown the first women in Scotland to win?
16 For which bakery product is Kirriemuir well known?
17 Which food or drink-related industry is associated with Alloa?
18 In which year was low-calorie Irn-Bru introduced to the market?
19 What is the name of the oldest surviving brewery in Scotland?
20 Which brewing company supplied ale to Bonnie Prince Charlie's troops in 1745?
21 What drink does the song about Campbeltown Loch celebrate?
22 Around which food does the Edinburgh/Glasgow vinegar/sauce debate revolve?
23 What is Dunsyre Blue?
24 Which whisky name was registered by James Logan Mackie?
25 What kind of food is a 'Pentland Squire'?

Answers: p187

General Knowledge 28

1 Where is the largest refinery for North Sea oil in Scotland?
2 In which century was the Thistle Chapel built?
3 North of which island is the island of South Rona?
4 Which was the first river in Europe to have a passenger turbine steamer service?
5 In which year was Scottish Enterprise formed?
6 In which loch is Davaar Island?
7 Where was Sir Malcolm Rifkind born?
8 Where is the East Lothian home of the Earl of Wemyss and March?
9 What is the name of the oilfield where the first major oil find was made in the North Sea?
10 The first edition of which reference book was edited by Andrew Findlater?
11 In which year did the *Braer* tanker break up off the coast of Shetland?
12 Which trade founded the first Co-operative Society in Britain in 1769, and where?
13 Which Scot was an official war artist in 1916 and again in 1939?
14 What was the name given to the fighting flag of the craftspeople of Edinburgh?
15 Which Scottish university botanic garden was established in 1971?
16 Which American newspaper was started by the Scot, James Gordon Bennet, in the nineteenth century?
17 Name the longest-serving Communist MP in British history.
18 Of which society was Lady Isobella Bishop the first lady fellow?
19 Which train won the Race to the North from London to Aberdeen in 1895?
20 Where was sculptor David Mach born?
21 Who took part in a 'Right to Work' demonstration in 1972?
22 Where is the ancient coronation site of the kingdom of Dalriada?
23 Name the author of *Rodney Stone*, published in 1896.
24 Who painted *The Cottar's Saturday Night* in 1854?
25 What military invention was devised by Patrick Ferguson in the eighteenth century?

Answers: p187

Heroes & Villains 2

1   Sir Patrick Manson carried out pioneering research on the cause of malaria and was one of the founders of the London School of Tropical Medicine. What was his nickname?

2   Who was the Scot appointed as the first director of the United Nations Food and Agriculture Organization in 1945?

3   He was a thieving cabinet-maker from Edinburgh, executed for his crimes. What was his name?

4   What is the name of the former manager of Celtic football club who died in 1985?

5   What nickname was given to the mystery triple killer who struck fear into the area around the Barrowlands in Glasgow in the 1960s?

6   Name the Scots climber who founded the Glencoe Mountain Rescue Team.

7   How did Captain Porteous die?

8   Who was the first European to cross the Rockies to the Pacific Ocean?

9   Which one of the evil partnership of Burke and Hare escaped the hangman's noose?

10 Name the sailor who was put ashore in a faraway place by William Dampier.

11 Who was killed at Kirk o' Field?

12 Which Scottish saint is thought to have been the teacher of St Kentigern?

13 Who starved Alexander Ramsay of Dalhousie to death in the dungeon of Hermitage Castle?

14 Where is Robert the Bruce believed to have spent his time in exile from 1306 to 1307?

15 What was the profession of explorer Mungo Park?

16 Which religious leader was responsible for the deaths of Patrick Hamilton and George Wishart?

17 Name the explorer who discovered Mount Erebus.

18 This Tayside man's notoriety stemmed not from his sins but from his poetry. What was his name?

19 What is the name of the airport worker who tackled one of the suspects in the 2007 terror attack on Glasgow International Airport?

20 With which events in Scottish history is the name of Patrick Sellar associated?

21 What was the name of the founder of the Boy's Brigade?

22 Name the judge, notorious for his harsh sentencing, who presided over the trial of Deacon Brodie.

23 For what is Sir Robert Alexander Watson-Watt remembered?

24 Who killed the Sheriff of Lanark in 1297?

25 Who was the first man to cycle from Dumfries to Glasgow?

Answers: p188

Life & Works of Robert Burns

1   'Sae rantingly, sae wantonly,
    Sae dantonly gaed he:
    He play'd a spring and danced it round,
    Below the gallows-tree.'
    About whom did Robert Burns write these words?
2   What was the name of Burns's father?
3   Where was Highland Mary born?
4   How old was Jean Armour when she married Robert Burns?
5   Who was 'Bonie Lesley'?
6   What was the name of Robert Burns's father's farm?
7   Who was 'Souter Johnnie'?
8   What was the name of the farm occupied by Robert Burns and his family after his marriage?
9   In which year did Robert Burns die?
10 In which year did Burns's father die?
11 What relation was Mrs John Begg to Robert Burns?
12 Which of Burns's legitimate children survived the longest?
13 Who was 'Holy Willie'?
14 To whom did Burns dedicate 'The Cottar's Saturday Night'?
15 Who was 'the Bonie Lass of Albanie'?
16 Where was the first Burns Club to be formally constituted?
17 Which poet scathingly referred to 'Burnomania' in a satirical poem, written in 1811?
18 What was the name of Robert Burns's mother?
19 Where did Burns nearly emigrate to in 1786?
20 As what did Burns find employment in Dumfries?
21 Who was the mother of Burns's first illegitimate child?
22 In which year did Burns move to Dumfries?
23 When did Burns make his Highland tour?
24 What was the name of the collection of songs and music which Burns edited?
25 Where was the farm leased by Burns and his brother after the death of their father?

Answers: p188

Scotland's Coastline

1   Travelling along the coast road from Elie to Anstruther, what is the name of the first village you pass through?
2   On which firth is Bo'ness situated?
3   Which town on the Solway Firth is a haven for painters and craftspeople?
4   What is the name of the bay upon which Creetown is situated?
5   Which fishing port lies just south-east of St Abb's?
6   Which major seaside town lies just to the south of Prestwick?
7   Which island is more northerly: Eigg or Muck?
8   Name the loch upon which Ullapool is situated.
9   What is the name of the bay upon which the fishing town of Buckie is situated?
10 Travelling from Oban to Colonsay by car ferry, where would you land?
11 Which famous lighthouse lies off the east coast, south-east of the town of Arbroath?
12 What is the name of the stretch of water between the islands of Skye and Raasay?
13 On which firth is the town of Oban situated?
14 Where on the Lothian Coast is Eagle Rock?
15 Which town south of Mallaig is famed for its beautiful sandy beaches?
16 Which coastal town is situated at the mouth of the River South Esk?
17 Which island in the Firth of Clyde provided a source of granite for curling stones?
18 Name the burgh in Lothian which stands below the two Forth Bridges.
19 What is the name of the castle, once the seat of the Black Douglas family, which lies to the east of North Berwick?
20 Where, on the east coast, did artist Joan Eardley find inspiration for many landscape paintings?
21 What do St Abb's Head and the Bass Rock have in common?
22 In which castle on the south-west coast did Robert the Bruce live as a child?
23 Which east coast bay, a short walk from Gullane, is an important nature reserve?
24 In which town in the south-west did the artist Jessie M. King live?
25 What is the name of the volcanic hill at North Berwick?

Answers: p189

General Knowledge 29

1 Which organizations were responsible for maintaining many of the roads in southern Scotland in the nineteenth century?

2 In which city were the Camperdown Works situated?

3 In which decade did the first Cranston's Tearoom open?

4 Against which English king did James IV declare war in 1513?

5 From which document does the following extract come? 'It is not for glory or riches or honour that we fight, but only for liberty . . .'

6 Where is the Archeolink Prehistory Park?

7 Where was the *Cutty Sark* built?

8 Which football club from the west of Scotland was founded in 1868?

9 Which castle in East Lothian has a distinctive round tower?

10 In which Scott novel will you encounter the Laird of Dumbiedykes?

11 What was manufactured by J. & P. Coats?

12 What kind of agricultural machine was invented by Patrick Bell?

13 Which Scottish king was killed at the Battle of Alnwick?

14 Name the photographer who published a set of lithographs entitled *Sketches of Scenery in Perthshire* in 1821.

15 What was the real name of the woman who wrote *Meg Dod's Cookery*?

16 What was the profession of James Keir?

17 What is the name of the architect of the Scottish Parliament Building?

18 Name the Scots philosopher who wrote about the death of David Hume.

19 Which party did Jim Sillars represent as an MP?

20 Which Scottish footballer and manager published an autobiography entitled *No Half Measures*?

21 Who built the *Charlotte Dundas*?

22 Who collaborated with Charles Rennie Mackintosh on his designs for the Cranston Tearooms?

23 Where was the sculptor George Wyllie born?

24 In which year did the North British Railway open between Edinburgh and Berwick-upon-Tweed?

25 In which month is St Serf's Day?

Answers: p189

Mountains & Hills

1. Which loch does Ben Slioch in Ross and Cromarty overlook?
2. What is a Munro?
3. What is the second highest mountain in the Cairngorms?
4. Where are the Five Sisters?
5. Which mountain overlooks the town of Callander?
6. What is the name of the mountain overlooking Spittal of Glen Muick?
7. How high is Ben Nevis?
8. Where is Beinn Nuis?
9. Which mountain is haunted by 'the Big Grey Man'?
10. What range of hills lies to the north of Glasgow?
11. What is the most northerly Munro?
12. There is one Ben Vorlich overlooking Loch Sloy, close to Tarbet. Where is the other one?
13. What does Ben More mean?
14. Which loch stands in the shadow of Ben Lawers?
15. Which mountain is sometimes called 'the Sugar Loaf'?
16. Which mountain range contains four out of five of Britain's highest mountains?
17. What is the name of the mountain system of which the Cairngorms are a part?
18. What is the name of the second-highest mountain in Scotland?
19. What is the name of the highest peak in the Black Cuillins?
20. What separates the North West Highlands and the Grampians?
21. Which mountain in Scotland has a feature called *Sgriob na Cailleach* (Old Woman's Furrow)?
22. Where are the Sow of Atholl and the Boar of Badenoch?
23. What is a Corbett?
24. In which part of Scotland is Ben Wyvis?
25. What does *Buchaille Etive Mor* mean?

Answers: p190

History 4

1 Which Second World War commando hero was described by Winston Churchill as 'the handsomest man who ever cut a throat'?

2 Who was called 'the father of Scotland's parliament'?

3 Where was Alexander III crowned?

4 In which year did Mary, Queen of Scots, marry Darnley?

5 Who was the first heretic to be burned in Scotland?

6 When was the Treaty of Perth between Norway and Scotland?

7 When was the Battle of Harlaw?

8 In which year was the Marquis of Montrose executed?

9 Who became king after the death of David II?

10 Who was burned at St Andrews in 1546?

11 In which year was the Kilbrandon Report published?

12 Which king founded the Court of Session?

13 In which year was the First Book of Discipline drawn up?

14 Which king of Scotland died at Jedburgh in 1165?

15 Who was declared king of Scotland by the Award of Berwick?

16 Which Sottish king was captured by the English at Neville's Cross and held to ransom?

17 In which century did Shetland come under Scottish rule?

18 In which year was the Stone of Destiny finally (officially) returned to Scotland?

19 Who was the last of the Celtic kings of Scotland?

20 Which historical battle anniversary was marked in April 1996?

21 Between which two kings was the Treaty of Abernethy drawn up in 1072?

22 Which punitive act was passed by the English parliament in 1705 to force Scotland's acceptance of the Treaty of Union?

23 Who was defeated at the Battle of Annan in 1332?

24 What grisly portent of doom was placed on the table at 'the Black Dinner' at Edinburgh Castle in 1440?

25 In which year was Edinburgh Castle taken by Covenanters?

Answers: p190

Holy People & Holy Places 2

1 What is the name of the founder of the Iona Community?
2 Where was the missionary and explorer David Livingstone born?
3 Where is St Columba's Cave?
4 Which ecclesiastical landmark in Glasgow was designed by Alexander 'Greek' Thompson?
5 Where was Patrick Hamilton burned at the stake?
6 In which century did St Serf live?
7 When did St John Ogilvie die?
8 Who is the patron saint of Paisley?
9 On which island was St Donan killed?
10 Who is the patron saint of Bute?
11 With which other country apart from Scotland is St Andrew associated?
12 To which saint is Candida Casa dedicated?
13 Who was the first Scot to become Archbishop of Canterbury?
14 Who was the mother of St Kentigern?
15 Which prominent Edinburgh clergyman announced his retiral in 2000?
16 Which Scottish saint became Bishop of Lindisfarne?
17 Who is the patron saint of Fife?
18 Which Scottish architect designed the new Coventry Cathedral in the 1950s?
19 Who wrote a biography of St Columba in the seventh century?
20 What is the name of the Scotswoman who became the first female chaplain to the Queen in 1991?
21 From which century does St Rule's Tower in St Andrews date?
22 Which cathedral was founded by St Gilbert of Moray, Bishop of Caithness?
23 In which century did St Fillan live?
24 Where did St Cuthbert die?
25 In which decade was the Central Mosque in Glasgow completed?

Answers: p191

General Knowledge 30

1   In which decade was the Dunning Report on the Scottish examination system produced?

2   What date is Tailie Day?

3   Who led Scotland's rugby team to their best-placed finsh in the history of the RBS Six Nations Championship in 2006?

4   Where can you visit the Royal Yacht *Britannia*?

5   How many ships does the National Lighthouse Board of Scotland own?

6   Where were the public records of Scotland stored during World War II?

7   For what medical purpose was birch-leaf tea drunk in the Highlands in olden days?

8   What was the primary function served by Blackness Castle in the sixteenth century?

9   What is the name of the outpost of the Edinburgh Royal Botanic Garden that is situated at Dunoon?

10 Where does the Earl of Aberdour live?

11 Where was the explorer William Balfour Baikie born?

12 Which Scot invented 'noctovision'?

13 On which small island is Scotland's first community-owned, grid-connected windfarm?

14 Who was the eighteenth-century leader of the Society of the Friends of the People in Scotland, campaigning for a parliament chosen by the people?

15 With which 'school' of Scottish fiction was the writer John Watson associated?

16 From which country did intense competition arise to Scotland's jute industry?

17 By what other name is Icolmkill more commonly known?

18 Name the well-known Dundee grocer who started a chain of shops throughout Scotland.

19 At the head of which loch does the village of Killin stand?

20 Which former Conservative MP (now deceased) lived at Fordell Castle?

21 From which part of Scotland does the Gordon clan come?

22 Which Banffshire town has 'Mare Mater' as its motto?

23 Which order of monks now lives at Nunraw Abbey?

24 What were Kingshouses?

25 What was/is a 'makar'?

Answers: p191

Wildlife 2

1   What is the name of the only poisonous snake to be found in Scotland?
2   Which animal, now rare in Scotland, is also known as the tree weasel?
3   Which large member of the umbrella-flowered parsley family, introduced to this country as an ornamental plant, has now become a serious nuisance in many parts of Scotland, threatening other species of wildflower?
4   Which part of Scotland has its own sub-species of wren?
5   Which animal, inhabiting the most lonely and inaccessible places in Scotland, is seldom seen during the day?
6   What is the name of the bird reserve on North Uist?
7   Which island is home to the second-largest colony of gannets in the UK?
8   Where is the largest blanket bog in Europe?
9   Where in Scotland is the largest gannet colony in the world?
10 In which part of Scotland does the crested tit breed?
11 What colour are the flowers of *Primula scotica*?
12 In which part of Scotland can *Primula scotica* be found?
13 Where are the best places in Scotland to view the sea eagle?
14 Which is larger; the golden eagle or the sea eagle?
15 By what other name is the sea eagle known?
16 What is the largest gull found in Scotland?
17 In which century is it thought that the Caledonian bear became extinct?
18 What is the most numerous auk found in Scotland?
19 What is Scotland's largest seabird?
20 Where is the Fowlsheugh RSPB reserve?
21 Where in Scotland can Britain's largest colony of fulmars be found?
22 Where in Scotland can Britain's largest population of breeding eider ducks be found?
23 What is a 'bonxie'?
24 Which nature reserve in Scotland celebrated its fiftieth birthday in 2001?
25 What is the most numerous seal found in Scotland?

Answers: p192

1   Which castle in Scotland is supposed to have a secret chamber, where the ghost of an ancient lord plays cards with the Devil for eternity?

2   What sort of ghostly phenomenon haunted a family in Rerrick in the eighteenth century?

3   What was customarily laid on the chest of a dead body awaiting burial, with the intent of keeping evil spirits away?

4   What could a cabbage plucked on Hallowe'en tell a young woman about her future husband?

5   Why was it believed unlucky to cut a baby's nails with scissors?

6   Why should new shoes never be placed on the table?

7   With which seer was the Queen of the Fairies said to have fallen in love?

8   Where is the ghost of Bluidy Mackenzie said to haunt?

9   What was the name of the mythological giant of Ben Ledi?

10   Complete the following couplet of weather lore: 'Ne'er cast a cloot . . .'

11   In times gone by, why might a suspected murderer be made to touch the corpse of the victim?

12   What is the 'holy ghost' that haunts St Rule's Tower in St Andrews?

13   Complete the following proverb: 'The Deil's bairns hae aye . . .'

14   In some parts of Scotland it was believed to be a bad omen to hear a dog howling in the night. What did it mean?

15   What was a 'Devil's Claw'?

16   Which historical event is said to have been prophesied by Thomas the Rhymer with the following lines?

'Between Seton and the sea
 Mony a man that day shall dee.'

17   In which century did the fear of witchcraft grow to such an extent that it became a capital offence?

18   What are the Mermaid's Tears of Iona, said to have been shed by a mermaid who had fallen in love with a saint?

19   Why would windows and doors be opened in a house where a death had recently taken place?

20   Why was rocking an empty cradle believed to be unlucky?

21   Which royal figure is said to haunt Linlithgow Palace?

22   Which Scottish mountain is haunted by a 'Big Grey Man'?

23   Which hidden close in Edinburgh is believed to be haunted by a child victim of the plague?

24   What kind of ghost is said to haunt Sandwood Bay in Sutherland?

25   Which famous Scottish castle is supposed to be haunted by a woman with no tongue?

Answers: p192

ANSWERS

ANSWERS

	General Knowledge 1		Industry 1
1	Loch Tummel	1	Linen
2	45	2	Aberdeen and Dundee
3	The nineteenth century	3	Glasgow
4	Slains Castle	4	Cotton
5	Wanlockhead	5	Speyside
6	Engineering	6	The Carse of Gowrie
7	Skye	7	Kilmarnock
8	Glamis	8	Perth
9	Fortingall	9	Bell and Dewar
10	Near Inver	10	Thomas Lipton
11	Aberdeen	11	Taynuilt
12	The Strathspey Railway	12	Tennents
13	Comrie lies on the Highland Boundary Fault	13	Textiles
		14	Fochabers
14	Elgin Cathedral	15	A jute mill
15	Durness	16	Clydebank
16	Kilmuir, Skye	17	1961
17	Robert McAlpine	18	Fife
18	The Church of St Mary, Haddington	19	Coal mining and salt-panning
		20	West Lothian
19	*The Name of the Rose*	21	1992
20	*Comet*	22	1963
21	Sir Henry Raeburn	23	A £10 million international innovation prize for advances in wave and tidal energy
22	Dalbeattie		
23	Sir Walter Scott		
24	Skibo Castle	24	There were two different St Rollox Works both existing close to each other but owned by different organizations: a chemical works and a railway works
25	Whitelee Windfarm, Eaglesham Moor, south of Glasgow		
		25	Dundee

Food & Drink 1

1 Smoked haddock
2 A soft, white curd cheese
3 A sheep's stomach
4 The Arbroath smokie, a smoked haddock
5 Forfar
6 Neeps (turnips) and chappit tatties (mashed potatoes)
7 Barley
8 Beef (shin bone)
9 A loaf baked with dried fruit
10 Hogmanay/New Year
11 Traquair Ale
12 The peat in the water
13 A measure of alcohol (about one pint)
14 The brewery
15 Herring
16 Oatmeal, honey, water and whisky
17 A kind of toffee, made with sugar, butter and treacle
18 Water of life (whisky)
19 A sweet a blob of dark mint toffee, made in Jedburgh
20 A mixture of potatoes and onions cooked slowly in a pan with meat scraps
21 Crab
22 Cranachan
23 Ayrshire
24 Aberdeen Angus
25 Salt

Television Trivia

1 Shieldinch
2 *Chewin' the Fat*
3 Gordon Ramsay
4 Richard Wilson
5 The Reverend I.M. Jolly
6 BBC 1
7 Ally McCoist
8 Kirsty Wark
9 John Leslie
10 Sheena Macdonald
11 *Reporting Scotland*
12 Mr Mackay
13 Sport
14 Dr Who
15 Plockton
16 Edinburgh
17 Robbie Coltrane
18 Aberdeen
19 John Laurie
20 Maggie Bell
21 Ardverikie Estate
22 Dr Cameron
23 John Byrne
24 Joe McFadden
25 Russell Hunter

General Knowledge 2

1 Devorguilla, wife of John Balliol and mother of King John Balliol
2 Queen Mary's House, Jedburgh
3 Fossil hunting
4 David Wilkie
5 A statue of an otter
6 Mauchline
7 Andrew Carnegie
8 Rab C. Nesbitt
9 Perth
10 A walking trail that criss-crosses the Kintyre peninsula
11 Irvine
12 Prestonpans
13 The Eildon Hills
14 St Mary's Loch
15 The Coats family
16 Humbie
17 The Cathedral of the Isles, Millport
18 The 1960s
19 The Society in Scotland for the Propagation of Christian Knowledge
20 James IV
21 Scapa Flow
22 Grampian
23 95 miles
24 There is a hydro in each of these towns.
25 The Brahan Seer

Poetry 1

1 John Barbour
2 William Dunbar
3 'Sir Patrick Spens'
4 Edwin Muir
5 George Mackay Brown
6 Liz Lochead
7 *Poems, Chiefly in the Scottish Dialect*
8 'Wallace'
9 John Davidson
10 Sorley Maclean
11 Robert Fergusson
12 Robert Garioch
13 James Graham, Marquis of Montrose
14 Hugh MacDiarmid
15 Agnes Maclehose
16 William Edmonstoune Aytoun
17 Edinburgh
18 James I
19 Robert Louis Stevenson
20 Carol Ann Duffy
21 Ettrick
22 Hamish Henderson
23 Hugh MacDiarmid
24 Norman MacCaig
25 *The Vision of Cathkin Braes*

ANSWERS

Wildlife 1

1   *Cirsium vulgare*
2   'Horse of the woods'
3   Heather shoots
4   Mink
5   Red deer
6   Juniper
7   Goose (in particular, the barnacle goose and the Greenland white-fronted goose)
8   A stretch of low-lying land by the shore, often a haven for wild flowers
9   Japan
10 Loch Garten
11 The 1950s
12 The grey squirrel is larger
13 The Tay and the Spey
14 When the hare is losing its white winter coat and remaining white hairs mingle with the brown hairs of its summer coat, its fur can take on a bluish tinge.
15 In the western Highlands
16 A butterfly
17 Loch Lomond
18 The National Nature Reserve of Beinn Eighe
19 Birch
20 *Pinus sylvestris*
21 The European beaver
22 St Kilda
23 The Scottish crossbill
24 The Moray Firth
25 The polecat

Life & Works of Sir Walter Scott

1   The High School
2   Paralysis of his right leg
3   1803
4   Robert, John, Daniel and Tom
5   Robert Burns
6   Effie Dean
7   Sandy Knowe
8   12
9   The Duchess of Wellington
10 The sixteenth century
11 Ashestiel
12 1814
13 'Old Mortality'
14 The coronation of George IV
15 Jonathan Oldbuck
16 Mons Meg
17 *St Ronan's Well*
18 1797
19 Charlotte Charpentier
20 *Götz von Berlichingen*
21 *The Siege of Malta*
22 *The Fair Maid of Perth*
23 Jane Jobson
24 Two
25 James and John Ballantyne

General Knowledge 3

1 His brother Henry, Cardinal of York

2 The Black Watch, the Argyll and Sutherland Highlanders, the Royal Highland Fusiliers, the Highlanders, and the former Royal Scots and the King's Own Scottish Borderers (amalgamated in 2006 as the Royal Scots Borderers)

3 St Oran

4 1507

5 MacDonald

6 Old Jock Gray

7 Allan Pinkerton

8 The Dean Gallery

9 1637, St Giles Cathedral, Edinburgh

10 George Buchanan

11 Prestwick

12 He drowned before it was completed.

13 He trained as a goldsmith and jeweller.

14 The Kingdom of Dalriada

15 Greenock

16 The Marquis of Montrose

17 Sir George Mackenzie

18 Preston Mill, East Lothian

19 Ettrick

20 Ayr

21 Duns

22 Edinburgh

23 Edinburgh

24 Scottish Qualifications Authority

25 Michael Kelly

Around & About in Scotland 1

1 Glencoe

2 Buchan Ness

3 Dundee

4 St Machar's Cathedral, Aberdeen

5 St Kilda

6 In the North Sea (they are oilfields).

7 Shetland

8 Achnacarry

9 Stirling

10 Near Pitlochry

11 Blackford Hill, Edinburgh

12 By Stirling castle

13 A waterfall

14 Tobermory Bay, the Isle of Mull

15 Pitlochry

16 New Lanark

17 Cromarty

18 Drumelzier

19 Dundee

20 The Lake of Menteith, Perthshire

21 Murrayfield, Edinburgh

22 Croick Church

23 Wanlockhead

24 Dumfries and Galloway (Kirkcudbrightshire)

25 Rannoch Moor

ANSWERS

ANSWERS

Law & Order

1. Assault of a person in his or her own home
2. Not proven
3. 1965
4. The Court of Session
5. 1996
6. Housebreaking and vandalism
7. Three years
8. The Children's Panel
9. Henry John Burnett
10. Madeleine Smith
11. Saughton
12. Robbery with violence
13. Poisoning his wife
14. The Lord Justice-General
15. They were strangled and burnt.
16. Carstairs
17. Advocate
18. Edinburgh
19. Barlinnie
20. The age at which marriage was legal without parental consent was lower in Scotland (16) than it was in England.
21. Kilmarnock
22. Lord Braxfield
23. (James Burnett) Lord Monboddo
24. Glasgow
25. Dean of Faculty

Music 1

1. The Communards
2. 'Pick Up the Pieces'
3. Frankie Miller
4. Japan
5. Simple Minds
6. Punk rock
7. Glasgow
8. Jim Kerr
9. Lonnie Donegan
10. Lulu
11. Elgin
12. Travis
13. The Poets
14. Annie Lennox
15. *Benny and Joon*
16. Lena Zavaroni
17. 'Ally's Tartan Army'
18. Baker Street
19. Glasgow
20. 1990
21. The Sensational Alex Harvey Band
22. Ultravox
23. Jim Diamond
24. Fish
25. 1975

Holy People & Holy Places 1

1   St Margaret
2   St Mungo
3   The twelfth century
4   St Aidan
5   St Giles Cathedral
6   30 November
7   John Knox
8   St Mirren
9   Fife
10 Rosslyn Chapel
11 Culross, Fife
12 St Andrews
13 Eskdalemuir
14 Thomas Chalmers
15 David I
16 St Magnus
17 Cistercian
18 Archbishop Kennedy
19 Iona
20 Borders
21 John Ogilvie
22 Glasgow Cathedral
23 The thirteenth century
24 Cambuskenneth Abbey
25 The Bass Rock

General Knowledge 4

1   Edinburgh
2   Edwin Morgan
3   Keir Hardie
4   a) 1965
5   Tay, Spey, Clyde, Tweed
6   It must be made from virgin Scottish wool, spun, dyed and handwoven in the Outer Hebrides
7   The National Party of Scotland
8   c) 1969
9   Loch Katrine
10 It was carried from place to place by runners to call clansmen to battle.
11 1746
12 *Doutelle*
13 They were all friends or sweethearts of Robert Burns.
14 c) 1832
15 Eigg
16 1964
17 David Tennant
18 The pine marten
19 Between Jura and Scarba
20 During the reign of Kenneth McAlpin
21 1297
22 Shinty
23 Chris Guthrie
24 William Blackwood, William Chambers, William Collins
25 John Maclean

History 1

1. 1320
2. 1951
3. Glenfinnan
4. 1567
5. The Ninth Legion
6. James VII
7. 1788
8. 1460
9. Macbeth
10. Duncan I
11. Macbeth
12. 1296
13. Carisbrooke Castle
14. Margaret, Queen of Scotland
15. Fotheringay
16. John Graham of Claverhouse, Viscount Dundee ('Bonnie Dundee')
17. 1542
18. The fifteenth century
19. 1328
20. William Wallace
21. 1698
22. The *Great Michael*
23. Sir John Stewart of Menteith
24. James VI
25. 30

Travel

1. 1897
2. The A70
3. Caledonian MacBrayne
4. b) 18 years
5. The Union Canal
6. Princes Street Station
7. 29
8. The Forth and Clyde Canal
9. 1890
10. Clackmannanshire Bridge
11. Suspension
12. 1842
13. Leuchars Junction
14. By ferry from Mallaig or on foot
15. Shetland (Mainland)
16. Glasgow, 1962
17. Cockbridge to Tomintoul
18. Across the Kintyre Peninsula, from Ardrishaig to Crinan
19. A74
20. Ayrshire
21. Glenshee
22. Cramond
23. The Kincardine Bridge
24. John o' Groats
25. The 1870s (1879)

Myth & Mystery, Magic & Superstition 1

1 The rowan tree
2 Morag
3 A devilish creature, associated with water
4 Tomnahurich
5 The Brahan Seer
6 A piece of silver
7 Aleister Crowley
8 To protect the dead person from evil spirits until he or she was given a Christian burial
9 Flannan Isle
10 Thomas the Rhymer
11 It was once believed that witches used eggshells as boats.
12 Black Donald the Devil
13 Findhorn
14 John Graham of Claverhouse ('Bonnie Dundee')
15 Curing consumption
16 Tam Dalyell
17 St Columba
18 A yellow monkey
19 Nine of diamonds
20 Green
21 The Lady of Lawers
22 A selkie (seal) could change itself into human form.
23 When the fairy flag is unfurled in battle, the enemies of the Macleod clan will see twice as many Macleods as there are in reality and the Macleods will not be defeated.
24 Iona
25 Brownies

General Knowledge 5

1 Ivor Cutler
2 *Reporting Scotland*
3 Mike Russell
4 Sean Connery
5 1947
6 b) The 1920s
7 2001
8 Lochdubh
9 Secretary-general of NATO
10 Edinburgh
11 The Netherlands
12 *Sunset Song, Cloud Howe* and *Grey Granite*
13 Pacific Quay on the Clyde, Glasgow
14 David Murray
15 The Liberal Democrats
16 The 1970s
17 Perth
18 Jimmy Somerville
19 1545
20 John Paul Jones
21 1989
22 William Smellie
23 Earl Haig
24 Gordonstoun
25 Sir Walter Scott

ANSWERS

Literature 1

1   The *Vital Spark*
2   Compton Mackenzie
3   William Robertson Nicoll
4   Sherlock Holmes
5   Thomas Carlyle
6   Sir Walter Scott
7   James Kelman
8   *How Late It Was How Late*
9   *The Man on My Back, A Year of Space* and *Fanfare for a Tin Hat*
10 Andrew Lang
11 *Dancing in the Streets*
12 'The Author of Waverley'
13 Iain Banks
14 George Douglas Brown
15 *Trainspotting*
16 Alasdair Gray
17 David Hume
18 The eighteenth century
19 Naomi Mitchison
20 *A Scots Quair*
21 John Buchan
22 Ian Rankin
23 Janice Galloway
24 *So Gaily Sings the Lark*
25 Kailyard fiction

Life & Works of John Buchan

1   Minister
2   Violet
3   From Pathhead
4   A fractured skull
5   Hutcheson's Grammar
6   His grandfather, John Masterton
7   *Chambers's Journal*
8   Lord Milner, High Commissioner for South Africa
9   *Blackwood's Magazine*
10 *The Thirty-Nine Steps*
11 24
12 Huntingtower
13 1935
14 *The Runagates Club* and *The Thirty-Nine Steps*
15 *Memory Hold-the-Door*
16 Four
17 *Prester John*
18 *Sick Heart River*
19 Alfred Hitchcock
20 'The Pilgrim Fathers'
21 Lord Tweedsmuir of Elsfield
22 *Sir Quixote of the Moors*
23 1916
24 Susan Grosvenor
25 1911

ANSWERS

	Aberdeen		General Knowledge 6
1	Her Majesty's Opera House	1	Oban
2	Union Terrace	2	Loch Lochy, Loch Oich and Loch Shiel
3	1963		
4	John Smith	3	Keathbank Mill, near Blairgowrie
5	Rubislaw Quarry		
6	Castle Hill, Gallowhill and St Catherine's Hill	4	1783
		5	Devorguilla
7	1593	6	In the Rhinns of Galloway
8	William Elphinstone, Bishop of Aberdeen	7	Glasgow (Buccleuch Street)
		8	Wanlockhead
9	1983	9	Barbara Mullen
10	Byron	10	Edinburgh
11	St Machar's Cathedral	11	b) the 1690s
12	The Aultoun Lily	12	David Livingstone
13	The eighteenth century	13	Cumbernauld
14	*The Aberdeen Journal*	14	Gudrun Ure
15	The Gordon Highlanders Regimental Museum	15	The opening of the new Scottish Parliament
16	The Castlegate	16	Billy Bremner
17	Aberdeen Joint Station	17	Ceres
18	Queen Victoria (statue)	18	James Bruce
19	'Bon Accord'	19	Alexander Naysmith
20	Dr Fenton Wyness	20	James VII and II
21	Hazlehead Park	21	The Earl of Morton
22	Alexander Keith	22	Deep Sea World, North Queensferry
23	His Majesty's Theatre		
24	Crombie Hall	23	Duns
25	The Gallowgate	24	Shipowner
		25	Sighting of the Loch Ness Monster

Feasts, Festivals & Fun

1 Kirkcaldy
2 September
3 A Viking longship
4 The Lammas Fair
5 August
6 The birthday of Robert Burns
7 At Hallowe'en
8 Fort William
9 September
10 Peebles
11 The Borders
12 St Andrews
13 11 January (the old New Year)
14 1 April
15 The first Monday of the New Year
16 Lanark
17 Glasgow
18 St Columba
19 By climbing Arthur's seat to wash their faces in the morning dew
20 30 November
21 Fastern's E'en
22 Glasgow's Mayfest
23 South Ronaldsay
24 Falkland
25 South Queensferry

Tunes That Made Them Famous

1 Bonnie Prince Charlie and Flora Macdonald
2 Lulu
3 The Corries
4 The Bay City Rollers
5 Robert Burns
6 Harry Lauder
7 Lady Carolina Nairne
8 Andy Stewart
9 Sheena Easton
10 Alexander Ewing
11 Alexander Hume
12 Gerry Rafferty
13 Lonnie Donegan
14 The Battle of Prestonpans
15 The Proclaimers
16 John Grieve
17 Wellies
18 Jarvis
19 Robert Burns
20 Lena Zavaroni
21 'I Belong to Glasgow'
22 'Boom Bang-a-Bang'
23 Jimmy Shand
24 Bonnie Prince Charlie
25 Robert Burns

Great Scots 1

1   A.S. Neill
2   Nigeria
3   Russia
4   The thirteenth century
5   Hugh Miller
6   St Margaret
7   David Hume
8   John Knox
9   Sir Henry Raeburn
10 Bonnie Prince Charlie
11 Katharine, Duchess of Atholl
12 Glasgow University
13 Allan Macdonald of Kingsburgh
14 Edwin Morgan
15 John Comyn of Badenoch
16 John Buchan
17 Alexander Graham Bell
18 George Buchanan
19 David I
20 William Thomson, Lord Kelvin
21 Lord Monboddo
22 Lewis Grassic Gibbon
23 Douglas
24 James Hutton
25 John Maclean

General Knowledge 7

1   Dornach
2   The *Solway Harvester*
3   James MacMillan
4   Belinda Robertson
5   A Scottish terrier
6   The Flannan Isles
7   Lord Balmerino
8   £431 million
9   The Royal Observatory
10 15 years old
11 b) 1727
12 The sixteenth century
13 'Flower of Scotland'
14 Sheena Easton
15 J.M. Barrie
16 Sarah Macauley
17 Milngavie, Fort William
18 Magnus Magnusson
19 1954
20 Taransay
21 Ben Cruachan
22 The Palace of Holyroodhouse
23 Fair Isle
24 E Coli outbreak
25 Margaret Ewing

ANSWERS

ANSWERS

Scotland & the Media

1. Andrew Neil
2. D.C. Thomson Ltd.
3. *The Glasgow Herald* (and before that, *The Glasgow Advertiser*)
4. *The Daily Record*
5. The 1970s
6. Sally
7. *The Scots Magazine*
8. *The Scotsman*
9. The eighteenth century
10. John Reith (Lord Reith)
11. *The Daily Record*
12. *The Sunday Express*
13. *The Sunday Post*
14. The eighteenth century
15. The Gaelic Broadcasting Committee
16. Television Limited
17. The 1930s
18. Aberdeen Journals Ltd
19. Glasgow
20. Aberdeen
21. *The Book Quiz*
22. Johnston Press
23. Gail Porter
24. Radio Clyde
25. 1961

Rugby

1. John Jeffrey
2. 1993
3. Three (1925, 1984, 1990)
4. David Sole
5. 1871
6. 1879
7. 1925
8. Her Royal Highness the Princess Royal
9. The Milne brothers (Ian, David and Kenneth)
10. Melrose
11. 20
12. Hawick
13. 1995
14. G.P.S. Macpherson
15. Inverleith
16. Most-capped player for Scotland
17. Melrose
18. 1883
19. Chris Paterson
20. 10 times
21. Longest-standing sponsor (Famous Grouse Whisky)
22. Three
23. 65
24. Tuberculosis
25. 2016 Olympic Games in Rio de Janeiro

ANSWERS

1   David Steel (Lord Steel)
2   In the despatch box in front of which the prime minister stands to speak
3   2007
4   Michael John Martin
5   Winnie Ewing
6   The Scottish Conservative and Unionist Party
7   53
8   Keir Hardie and R.B. Cunninghame Graham
9   1939
10 1950
11 33 per cent
12 First minister
13 James (Jimmy) Reid
14 1902–5
15 Sir Alec Douglas-Home
16 Edward Heath
17 John Swinney
18 Mike Russell
19 Iona
20 Transport minister
21 George Hamilton Gordon, 4th Earl of Aberdeen
22 Andrew Fletcher of Saltoun
23 Jimmy Reid
24 John Maclean
25 Iain Gray

1   Richard Holloway
2   The Happy Gang
3   Judge George Mackenzie
4   Aviemore, Kingussie, Pitlochry
5   For playing his pipes while under fire during the Normandy landings
6   Dr William Hunter
7   Collessie
8   An Teallach
9   The haggis
10 Celtic
11 Westray and Papa Westray
12 Strathclyde Country Park
13 Glen Shira
14 Warmer winter temperatures caused by global warming
15 Edinburgh Castle
16 1959
17 *Cracker*
18 Enric Miralles
19 Edinburgh
20 The red kite
21 Gruinard
22 John Smith
23 Aly Bain
24 Donnie McLeod
25 Sir William Arrol

ANSWERS

1 Charles Rennie Mackintosh
2 William Playfair
3 William Burn
4 Rothesay, Isle of Bute
5 Barry Gasson
6 John Thomas Rochead
7 A windowless one-room thatched cottage
8 William Blackie
9 A prehistoric building, round in shape, with tall sloping sides, probably built as both dwelling and defence for many people
10 David Bryce
11 Robert and James
12 Sir Basil Spence
13 James Craig
14 Donaldson's School (formerly Donaldson's Hospital)
15 William Leiper
16 Scotland Street School
17 A small, two-roomed house
18 William Bruce
19 Sir Robert Lorimer
20 Culzean Castle
21 Queens Cross Church
22 Robert Mylne
23 James Gillespie Graham
24 Thomas Hamilton
25 William Adam

1 The Dundee Repertory Theatre Company
2 Mary Slessor
3 Samuel Bell
4 Camperdown Park
5 Step Row
6 The old Tay Ferry
7 1190
8 Thomas Bouch
9 Queen Victoria
10 The *Terra Nova*
11 The *Unicorn*
12 Mills Observatory
13 June
14 Liz McColgan
15 The Average White Band
16 William the Lion
17 The Arabs
18 1881
19 Mary Shelley's Frankenstein
20 1651
21 The 1830s
22 The Baxters
23 The Coxes
24 The Logie Works
25 Alexander Riddoch

Bonnie Prince Charlie

1. 31 December 1720
2. 1725
3. 1735
4. Northern Italy
5. 1744
6. Admiral Roqueville
7. They were the seven men who helped Charles in his period of hiding after Culloden and prior to his escape from Scotland.
8. The Tower of London
9. Lieutenant-general Henry Hawley
10. Francis Strickland
11. Prestonpans
12. Edinburgh Castle
13. November
14. December
15. The capture of Carlisle
16. 1745
17. Derby
18. Five months
19. Six days
20. 1753
21. 1750
22. Archibald Cameron
23. 1760
24. Princess Louise of Stolberg
25. Vittorio Alfieri

General Knowledge 9

1. 1971
2. Peterhead
3. Glasgow
4. Alastair Dunnett
5. William Collins
6. Scottish country dancing – the Royal Scottish Country Dance Society
7. Sir Alexander Fleming
8. Lighthouse engineer
9. Thomas Telford
10. The thirteenth century
11. Shipping
12. The Regent Morton
13. 1812
14. The Scottish Cooperative Wholesale Society
15. Rhododendrons
16. The National Library of Scotland
17. Bishop Wardlaw
18. James Chalmers
19. James Francis Stewart, the Old Pretender
20. Greyfriars Churchyard
21. The first decade of the seventeenth century (1603)
22. Aberdeen University
23. Leith
24. Plump, comely
25. 33 including the Scottish Council of Independent Schools

ANSWERS

Golf

1 Catriona Matthew
2 William Auchterlonie
3 1889
4 St Andrews
5 St Andrews
6 Machrihanish, Kintyre
7 Muirfield
8 1860
9 The Royal Burgess Golfing Society
10 James II
11 Sandy Lyle
12 Edinburgh
13 Willie Park Senior
14 1977
15 The 17th
16 Muirfield
17 Colin Montgomerie
18 Seven (Prestwick, St Andrews, Royal Musselburgh, Muirfield, Troon, Carnoustie, Turnberry)
19 Gleneagles
20 'Young Tom' Morris
21 'Young Tom' Morris
22 1988
23 1931
24 The King's
25 22

Films & Film Stars 1

1 Helen Mirren
2 John Hannah
3 Ewan McGregor
4 Dee Hepburn
5 Danny Boyle
6 Orkney
7 *When Eight Bells Toll*
8 *Comfort and Joy*
9 Knoydart
10 The Forth Rail Bridge
11 Glasgow
12 Bill Forsyth
13 Phyllis Logan
14 The sinking of the SS *Politician*
15 Begbie
16 Gordon Jackson
17 Ewan McGregor
18 William McIlvanney
19 Sean Connery
20 Rob Roy
21 Robbie Coltrane
22 Gavin Maxwell
23 John Gordon Sinclair
24 Miss Jean Brodie
25 *Whisky Galore*

The Borders

1 Chambers (William and Robert Chambers were both born in Peebles.)
2 King David I
3 William Adam (eighteenth century) and William Playfair (nineteenth century)
4 Melrose
5 The River Tweed and the River Teviot
6 Jedburgh Castle
7 Floors Castle
8 Riverside Park
9 Peebles
10 June
11 A museum
12 Eyemouth
13 Galashiels
14 James Hogg
15 Michael Scott
16 James (Jim) Clark
17 The eleventh century
18 Peebles
19 Five
20 Jedburgh
21 Kelso Abbey
22 Melrose Abbey
23 Innerleithen
24 Dryburgh Abbey
25 Drumelzier

General Knowledge 10

1 The 1870s
2 Famine
3 The reign of James II
4 The Black Death
5 For the Glasgow Exhibition of 1901
6 The eighteenth century
7 At a reception in his honour held at Holyrood House
8 The Edinburgh International Conference Centre
9 The 250th anniversary of the Battle of Culloden
10 Kinnaird Head
11 The Marquis of Queensberry (8th)
12 Andrew Wilson
13 Strathclyde University
14 James Mollison
15 Anti-nuclear campaigning
16 The Mull of Kintyre
17 Teaching
18 China
19 Westminster Abbey
20 Twice
21 Harry Lauder
22 Moira Shearer
23 Queen Victoria at Balmoral
24 Keith Schellenberg
25 EventScotland in partnership with VisitScotland

ANSWERS

ANSWERS

Industry 2

1 Proposals for a gold-mining operation
2 The jewellery industry (silversmiths)
3 1970
4 Sir James Hamilton
5 Publishing
6 The eighteenth century
7 Glasgow
8 Brora
9 Slate
10 Robert Owen
11 1838
12 1897
13 Blantyre
14 Robert Bald
15 Summer (July to September)
16 Drift nets
17 Failures of the potato crops
18 Glass
19 1711
20 1965
21 Mining
22 The 1870s
23 The Bank of Scotland
24 Paisley
25 Glasgow

Royalty

1 Prince Charles
2 Robert the Bruce
3 1649
4 Mary of Guise
5 Prince Edward, son of Edward I, future Edward II
6 1452
7 Falkland Palace
8 James IV
9 Anne
10 Malcolm III
11 1561
12 He was killed by an exploding cannon.
13 Margaret Tudor
14 James VI
15 Gruoch
16 1603
17 Charles I
18 1685
19 Son-in-law
20 Margaret Tudor
21 15 years old
22 Anne of Denmark
23 Alexander III
24 Rome
25 James I

Football 1

1 1975/6 season
2 Rangers
3 Celtic
4 Sir Matt Busby
5 102
6 There were riots after two drawn games between Celtic and Rangers.
7 1903/4
8 25
9 1990
10 Manchester United
11 Partick Thistle
12 Hibernian
13 Kenny Dalglish
14 1910
15 Jock Stein
16 Clydebank
17 Kenny Dalglish
18 Rangers
19 Alex Ferguson
20 Blue and white
21 Third Lanark
22 The 1940s and 50s
23 Second World War
24 Hearts
25 Celtic Park

General Knowledge 11

1 Vane Farm
2 The Forests of Caledon
3 Scottish Site of Special Scientific Interest
4 Eriskay and South Uist
5 St Kilda
6 Sheep cloned from embryo cells
7 Cockburnspath
8 Because of erosion of land by the sea which has destroyed some houses in the past and threatens further destruction
9 The Scottish deerhound
10 Lulu
11 *Monarch of the Glen*
12 Cranium
13 Wigtown
14 David I
15 19 years
16 Aberdeen
17 Tommy Sheridan
18 The Giant's Causeway
19 Glenfiddich
20 The 1990s
21 Blacksmith
22 The Paddy Meehan case
23 James Thin
24 King Robert II
25 Loch Fyne

ANSWERS

Dumfries & Galloway

	Art		Dumfries & Galloway
1	Joan Eardley	1	Thornhill
2	Portraiture	2	Greyfriars Monastery, Dumfries
3	Son	3	New Galloway
4	John Bellany	4	1988
5	George Wyllie	5	The statue of a ram
6	The Scottish Colourists	6	Langholm
7	Ian Hamilton Finlay	7	Broughton House
8	Edinburgh	8	The twelfth century
9	Peter Howson	9	The cotton industry
10	James Drummond	10	The River Urr
11	Edinburgh College of Art	11	Dundrennan Abbey
12	The Glasgow Boys	12	The River Ken
13	Frances (Fra) Newbery	13	Sanquhar
14	Margaret Macdonald Mackintosh	14	The sixteenth century
15	Anne Redpath	15	Whithorn (the Priory Museum)
16	Ken Currie	16	Two
17	William McTaggart	17	Keir
18	David Wilkie	18	Kirkcudbright
19	Eduardo Paolozzi	19	In the graveyard of the Church of St Michael, Dumfries
20	In a church in Edinburgh's Broughton Street	20	Threave Castle
21	The Glasgow Girls	21	Torthorwald
22	Sir Joseph Noel Paton	22	Wanlockhead
23	North Lands Creative Glass, Lybster	23	A hill
24	A.E. Hornel	24	Stranraer
25	Emilio Coia	25	Ecclefechan

Sport 1

1. David Wilkie
2. Jackie Stewart
3. Alan Wells
4. 2000
5. Jim Clark
6. Golf
7. St Andrews
8. Boxing
9. September
10. Stephen Hendry
11. Colin MacRae
12. American football
13. Sandy Lyle
14. Willie Carson
15. Paul Lawrie
16. Shirley Robertson
17. Liz McColgan
18. Long jump
19. Warrender
20. 1999
21. Chris Paterson
22. Stephen Hendry
23. East Stirling
24. 3 (team sprint, individual sprint, men's keirin)
25. 1985

General Knowledge 12

1. The 1930s
2. Wetsminster Abbey
3. The 1830s
4. Juan Fernandez
5. William Armstrong
6. The Admirable Crichton
7. The sixteenth century
8. The eighteenth century
9. The Educational Institute of Scotland
10. Lord advocate and solicitor-general for Scotland
11. The 1940s
12. John was William's uncle.
13. The Nobel Prize for Economics
14. Charles Macintosh
15. The Turin Exhibition
16. India
17. John was the younger.
18. Photographer
19. George Heriot
20. 1949
21. The Cuillins
22. 1977
23. The Royal Highland Show
24. Balfour Beatty
25. 1291

ANSWERS

1 A Gaelic harp
2 *I Don't Want a Lover*
3 Nicola Benedetti
4 Ravel
5 Scotch Snap
6 Roy Williams
7 The Corries
8 Wordless unaccompanied singing, for dancing
9 Accordion
10 Same home town (Auchtermuchty)
11 Midge Ure
12 Three
13 2/4
14 The Eurythmics
15 Scottish Opera
16 Reels
17 Judith Weir
18 Perthshire, near Dunkeld
19 Kenneth McKellar
20 Piano
21 Wet Wet Wet
22 Andy Stewart
23 Felix Mendelssohn
24 *Scottish Fantasy*
25 The fiddle

1 The Long Island
2 Scalpay
3 The MacNeills
4 1930
5 The Fairy Flag
6 Eigg
7 Kirkwall
8 Craignure
9 Staffa
10 Skye
11 Lochmaddy
12 Golf
13 Oronsay
14 Islay
15 Skye
16 Dervaig
17 Lewis
18 Kisimul Castle
19 Ben Mhor
20 Lighthouse
21 Achamore House Gardens
22 Jura (Barnhill)
23 Brodick Castle
24 North Ronaldsay
25 Sunken German fleet

Great Scots 2

1. Adam Ferguson
2. Robert Cunninghame Graham
3. Ludovic Kennedy
4. James Hogg
5. Thomas Chalmers
6. Chloroform
7. Sir Thomas Craig of Riccarton
8. Sir David Wilkie
9. *Mind*
10. Engineering
11. William Barclay
12. Jock Stein
13. Jackie Stewart
14. Veterinary surgeon
15. Helena Kennedy
16. Rob Roy MacGregor
17. John Kerr
18. Sir James Murray
19. Science (physics)
20. Chemist
21. The Independant Broadcasting Authority
22. Sir James Young Simpson
23. Hugh MacDiarmid
24. William Ramsay
25. Sir Alexander Fleming

General Knowledge 13

1. St Kilda
2. Charles Marjoribanks, the first MP for Berwickshire
3. Portpatrick
4. Six
5. Stan Laurel
6. Selkirk
7. Cooking oatcakes or small loaves
8. *The Fortunes of Nigel*
9. The 1760s
10. Protection in battle (It is a shield.)
11. Coffins
12. A shoemaker
13. Pitt the Elder
14. Colin Campbell of Glenure
15. A Scottish battleship
16. The reign of James III
17. The 1960s
18. By government
19. Edinburgh
20. 1567
21. April Fool's day
22. Wallace
23. George Wyllie
24. The nineteenth century
25. Bill Shankly

ANSWERS

Castles

1. Mainland Shetland
2. The Dukes and Earls of Sutherland
3. It is triangular in shape.
4. John Napier
5. Hepburn
6. Kilconquhar
7. The MacDonalds of Clan Ranald
8. As a youth hostel
9. Edinburgh Castle
10. George Heriot
11. Rothesay Castle
12. Niddry Castle
13. Yester Castle
14. Sinclair
15. The ghost of a French maid, burned for witchcraft
16. The Ogilvies
17. The sixteenth century
18. Tantallon Castle
19. Dollar
20. Unst
21. Castlebay, Barra
22. Sir Fitzroy Maclean
23. Threave Castle
24. The Isle of Skye
25. The nineteenth century

Literature 2

1. Robert Louis Stevenson
2. Hugh Miller
3. J.M. Barrie
4. John Galt
5. Neil Munro
6. Elgin
7. John Buchan
8. George MacDonald
9. William McIlvanney
10. James Kennaway
11. Ian Rankin
12. Sir Walter Scott
13. Archibald Constable
14. Dr Jekyll and Mr Hyde
15. Sir Walter Scott's unfinished memoir of his early life
16. 1767
17. Neil Gunn
18. *Blackwood's Edinburgh Magazine*
19. The 1830s
20. Elgin
21. John Hay Beith
22. Printing (as a compositor)
23. Chambers Harrap
24. Maurice Lindsay
25. *1984*

ANSWERS

Scottish Women

1 She worked in a jute mill.
2 Kinross and Perthshire
3 Mary Garden
4 Dame Muriel Spark
5 Elsie Inglis
6 10,000 metres
7 She disguised herself as a man, and was known throughout her career as James Barry.
8 She was an art teacher.
9 1979
10 Secretary of state, Scottish Office
11 Hannah Gordon
12 Hockey
13 Judith Weir
14 Three
15 Dave Stewart
16 Ena Baxter
17 Glasgow
18 Jenny Geddes
19 Elizabeth Blackadder
20 1965
21 Tibbie Shiel
22 Lary Carolina Nairne
23 Deborah Kerr
24 The thirteenth century (1251)
25 Myrtle Lillias Simpson

General Knowledge 14

1 The Royal Botanic Garden
2 Marjory
3 Lord Reith
4 The 1970s
5 Arthur Henderson
6 Sir David Patrick Maxwell Fyfe
7 Norman Lamont
8 Newark
9 Malcolm III was Duncan I's son.
10 James Mackay of Clashfern
11 The Nobel Prize for Medicine
12 Menzies
13 As a soprano
14 The nineteenth century
15 Tarlair
16 Alexander III
17 David Allan
18 1998
19 2000
20 Gordonstoun
21 Princes Street Gardens
22 David I
23 The seventeenth century
24 Duke of York
25 1918

Around & About in Scotland 2

1 Forres
2 Cambuskenneth Abbey
3 Oldmeldrum
4 Perth
5 Edinburgh
6 Edinburgh
7 Falkland Palace
8 East Linton
9 Shetland, the Mousa Broch
10 Skye
11 St Andrews
12 Between Loch Etive and Loch Linnhe
13 Paisley
14 A series of locks at Banavie, on the Caledonian Canal
15 Close to Innerpeffray Castle, near Crieff
16 Near Moffat
17 Tain
18 Orkney
19 Gruinard
20 Anstruther, Fife
21 The Shetlands
22 Blantyre
23 Kintail, Wester Ross
24 An ornate summerhouse with a pineapple shaped first floor, Airth, Stirlingshire
25 Glencoe

Science, Engineering, Invention & Innovation

1 The Rocket
2 1875
3 Robert Stevenson
4 A pneumatic tyre
5 James Watt
6 John Rennie senior and John Rennie junior
7 1757
8 John Dunlop
9 James Watt
10 The kaleidoscope
11 William Murdock
12 Kirkpatrick Macmillan
13 Bleaching powder
14 Four feet eight and a half inches
15 James Young
16 Thomas Nelson
17 The Roslin Institute, Penicuik
18 Lord Kelvin
19 The paddle-steamer built by William Symington
20 John Kerr
21 Professor Ian Wilmut
22 It was created from a frozen calf embryo, defrosted and implanted in a 'surrogate mother' cow.
23 1926
24 The Ultrasound scanning machine
25 Robert Stein

	Fife		General Knowledge 15
1	The fourteenth century	1	In the reign of Malcolm IV
2	King Robert the Bruce	2	Newhaven
3	Elie	3	The Battle of Tippermuir
4	The Lomond Hills	4	Glasgow International Airport
5	Leuchars	5	Ian Vallance
6	North Queensferry	6	The white rose
7	Pittenweem	7	*High Road*
8	St Andrews	8	Canongate
9	Coal mining and salt-panning	9	The nineteenth century
10	Culross	10	Grinding corn
11	Glenrothes	11	Wishaw
12	Dunfermline	12	The Gorbals, Glasgow
13	The oil industry	13	The Kelvin Hall, Glasgow
14	The fourteenth century	14	A record shop (in Edinburgh)
15	The Scottish Fisheries Museum	15	The 1790s
16	Leuchars Junction	16	Edinburgh
17	The linen industry	17	The weavers
18	Falkland	18	Henry Cockburn
19	Near Anstruther	19	John Maclean
20	St Andrews	20	John Buchan
21	Lochgelly	21	Peter Manuel
22	St Monans	22	Holy Island, Arran
23	Alexander III	23	The John Muir Trust
24	Culross	24	Adam Smith
25	Earlsferry	25	1736

ANSWERS

ANSWERS

	Where Were They Born?		Otherwise Known As . . .
1	Kirkcaldy, Fife	1	Hugh MacDiarmid, poet
2	Largo, Fife	2	Marie McDonald McLaughlin Lawrie
3	Inveraray, Argyll	3	Mary Campbell
4	Haddington, East Lothian	4	Thomas Glover
5	Turnberry, Ayrshire	5	Kirriemuir
6	Linlithgow Palace	6	Dunfermline
7	Perth	7	James VI
8	Edinburgh	8	Colin Campbell
9	Lossiemouth, Morayshire	9	James Scott Skinner
10	Glasgow	10	George Heriot
11	Kirkcaldy, Fife	11	Gardenstown
12	Edinburgh	12	Malcolm IV
13	Govan, Glasgow	13	Canmore
14	Edinburgh	14	Kirkcaldy
15	Blantyre, Lanarkshire	15	Jim Baxter
16	Bathgate, West Lothian	16	Musselburgh
17	Edinburgh	17	William I
18	Cardenden, Fife	18	John Balliol
19	Glasgow	19	Sir Walter Scott
20	Kirriemuir, Angus	20	Football players for Hibernian (Gordon Smith, Bobby Johnstone, Lawrie Reilly, Eddie Turnbull, Willie Ormond)
21	Dunblane, Perthshire	21	Bill McLaren
22	Edinburgh Castle	22	Edward I of England
23	Edinburgh	23	The name given to the 93rd Sutherland Highlanders defending Balaclava
24	Langholm, Dumfries and Galloway	24	Archibald, 5th Earl of Angus
25	Dunfermline	25	George Mackenzie, judge

Films & Film Stars 2

1   Sean Connery
2   Edinburgh
3   Robert Carlyle
4   Robbie Coltrane
5   *Four Weddings and a Funeral*
6   Pennan
7   Fulton Mackay
8   Tom Conti
9   Edinburgh
10 Billy Connolly
11 St Andrews (the West Sands)
12 *A Sense of Freedom*
13 Alastair Sim
14 James Robertson-Justice
15 Andrew Macdonald
16 1960
17 Ian Charleson
18 Ewan McGregor
19 Rikki Fulton
20 Will Fyffe
21 *Harry Potter and the Chamber of Secrets* (2002)
22 Stanley Baxter
23 Bill Douglas
24 Richard Hannay in *The Thirty-Nine Steps*
25 John Grierson

General Knowledge 16

1   Lord Reith
2   John Steell
3   Eat it (It is salted gannet.)
4   Soay sheep
5   James I
6   Glasgow
7   Hallowe'en
8   1974
9   The seventeenth century (1690)
10 The Bill of Rights
11 James VII
12 700 years
13 The First Bishops' War
14 The Countess of Mar
15 James III
16 James VII
17 St Kilda
18 Kenmore, Perthshire
19 Celtic
20 Madeleine Smith
21 1747
22 Govan
23 The Battle of Solway Moss
24 Robert Fergusson
25 Ewan McGregor

ANSWERS

Sport 2

1   Granite
2   St Andrews
3   Twelve
4   1889
5   Lanark Racecourse
6   Ice hockey
7   Motorcycle racing
8   Jackie Stewart
9   Ally McCoist
10 1968
11 Benny Lynch
12 John Higgins
13 Liz McColgan
14 Three
15 Stephen Hendry
16 St Andrews Rowing Club
17 Jim McLean
18 Hillend, Edinburgh
19 Braemar
20 Willie Carson
21 29 (11 gold, 7 silver, 11 bronze)
22 McLaren-Mercedes
23 30
24 The Royal and Ancient, St Andrews
25 Yacht races

Language

1   A toad or frog
2   A crow
3   Spend it: a bodle was a unit of currency.
4   Your throat
5   A short shift
6   False. 'Sic-like' means 'such as'.
7   It means don't worry, don't bother or don't trouble yourself.
8   No. 'To flit' means to move house.
9   Twilight, early evening
10 Idle chatter, gossip
11 Mud, muck, filth
12 Hips
13 Eat it. 'Parritch' is porridge.
14 A slice of cheese
15 False. It is a wasps' nest.
16 Girls and boys
17 No. 'Muckle gab' means big mouth.
18 A mole (blemish)
19 A shoemaker. A 'lapstane' was a stone upon which the leather was beaten to soften it.
20 Yes. 'Couthie' means kind, loving.
21 A broody hen
22 A weave and a rope
23 With a struggle
24 A coin (very small value)
25 Doric

Around Edinburgh & the Lothians

1   John Muir
2   Linlithgow Palace
3   Haddington
4   East Linton
5   The Tyne Water
6   East Fortune
7   The island of Inchcolm
8   Sir William St Clair
9   Newtongrange
10 Penicuik
11 North Berwick
12 The twelfth century
13 Calder house, Mid Calder
14 Livingston
15 The John Muir Country Park
16 Rosslyn Chapel
17 Bothwell Castle
18 Edinburgh
19 Sir Walter Scott
20 The shale oil industry
21 Glencorse
22 South Queensferry
23 The North Esk
24 Musselburgh
25 Mary, Queen of Scots

General Knowledge 17

1   The nineteenth century
2   The eighteenth century
3   Alexander Buchan
4   Newcastle, Berwick, Stirling, Perth
5   Matthew Boulton
6   James Bruce
7   The Scottish Home Rule Association
8   The SAS
9   Kenny Dalglish
10 The Orcs and the Cats
11 The SFA
12 The King's Own Scottish Borderers
13 James V
14 Cockburnspath
15 Commander-in-chief in Scotland
16 The eighteenth century
17 Berwick Rangers
18 Ayr
19 A riverside plain
20 Perthshire
21 1513
22 Victor and Barry
23 St Andrews
24 Muriel Gray
25 Queen Street Station and Central Station

Poetry 2

1. 'To a Haggis'
2. James Hogg
3. Robert Louis Stevenson
4. Lewis
5. Sydney Goodsir Smith
6. Hugh MacDiarmid
7. Sorley Maclean
8. Robert Burns
9. Orkney
10. Sir Walter Scott
11. Leadhills, Dumfries and Galloway
12. John Gibson Lockhart
13. 1920
14. Hugh MacDiarmid
15. Thomas Campbell
16. Edwin Muir
17. Andrew Young
18. Ian Hamilton Finlay
19. Liz Lochhead
20. Robert Louis Stevenson
21. James MacPherson
22. Teacher
23. Hugh MacDiarmid
24. James Hogg
25. Carol Ann Duffy

Central Scotland & Tayside

1. The Allan Water
2. Loch Katrine
3. Dollar Academy
4. Schiehallion
5. Auchterarder
6. Textiles: jute and flax
7. 1297
8. No
9. The River Ardoch and the River Teith
10. Fasque House
11. 'The Birks o' Aberfeldy'
12. The National Trust for Scotland
13. Moot Hill
14. The River Tummel
15. The children were eaten by wolves.
16. In Pullar's Dye Works in Perth
17. Ben Lawers
18. St Angus
19. The twelfth century
20. Dunkeld
21. Stirling University
22. Loch Earn
23. William Bruce
24. The eighteenth century
25. The Ochils

Life & Career of Sean Connery

1 1930
2 Joe
3 McLean
4 Thomas
5 He was discharged on medical grounds.
6 1981
7 Jason
8 Dustin Hoffman and Matthew Broderick
9 1965
10 Micheline
11 *Medicine Man*
12 King Richard
13 Stephan
14 *From Russia with Love*
15 *1991*
16 *No Road Back*
17 Golf
18 1962
19 *The Hill*
20 Diane Cilento
21 Malone, a Chicago policeman
22 *Murder on the Orient Express*
23 1983
24 *Indiana Jones and the Last Crusade*
25 *The League of Extraordinary Gentlemen*

General Knowledge 18

1 Jimmy Boyle and Hugh Collins
2 Mairi Hedderwick
3 Red, yellow and black
4 It was beneath the sand and was uncovered after a particularly bad storm blew the sand away.
5 Chairman of the Scottish Tourist Board
6 The 1960s
7 Stagecoach
8 James II
9 A four-pronged spear for catching salmon
10 A breed of sheep
11 Dougal Haston
12 Barbie
13 William Younger and William McEwan
14 The 1970s
15 Mining
16 It was the locomotive salvaged and put back into service after the Tay Bridge disaster.
17 Graeme Souness
18 As a composer
19 Allan Ramsay
20 The 1960s
21 W.Y. McGregor
22 Thomas Telford
23 Edinburgh
24 William of Orange was his son-in-law
25 1842

ANSWERS

ANSWERS

1 Viscount Haldane
2 He opposed the British government's involvement in the First World War.
3 Alexander Leslie
4 James VII and II and Anne Hyde
5 1923
6 1579
7 She was also accused of plotting against King James VI.
8 James Sharp
9 Queen Anne
10 1688
11 Mary of Modena
12 Falkirk
13 1580
14 1600
15 1930
16 1595
17 1822
18 The Wolf of Badenoch
19 Grantown-on-Spey
20 1716
21 The police and the tenants of Lord MacDonald
22 1567
23 1390
24 Montrose
25 1503

1 Arthur's Seat
2 The twelfth century
3 The Caledonian Hotel
4 The Royal Mile
5 The Flodden Wall
6 Princes Street
7 David Rizzio
8 Mary King's Close
9 The one o'clock gun, fired from the castle
10 The Edinburgh Military Tattoo
11 On the Royal Mile, in front of Parliament Square
12 Greyfriars Bobby
13 The eighteenth century
14 Portobello
15 The site of Princes Street Gardens
16 A lock-up shop (The Luckenbooths were situated in the Royal Mile, close to St Giles.)
17 The National Gallery of Scotland and the Royal Scottish Academy
18 Every two years
19 The Commonwealth Games, 1970
20 The Fringe
21 Mons Meg
22 At the top of Castle Hill, at the entrance to the castle esplanade
23 'Gardyloo!'
24 Robert Adam
25 The Dean Bridge

ANSWERS

	Politics 2		General Knowledge 19
1	Govan, Glasgow	1	Sir Arthur Conan Doyle
2	John Smith	2	The Uist Tramping Song
3	1934	3	Matilda
4	Henry McLeish	4	The vacuum flask
5	1945	5	St Andrews
6	Foreign secretary	6	McTavish
7	Mining	7	Sir Alexander Fleming
8	The Duchess of Atholl	8	Finland
9	Holyrood, Edinburgh	9	Three (James V, James VI and James VII)
10	George Hamilton Gordon, 4th Earl of Aberdeen	10	Margaret, the Maid of Norway
11	Alex Salmond	11	Alastair Maclean
12	56	12	The Cairngorms
13	Nine	13	The Bay City Rollers
14	Gordon Brown	14	Celtic
15	23 years (1974–97)	15	Coal and steel (He was chairman first of British Steel and then of the National Coal Board.)
16	1938	16	Napier University
17	Labour	17	Aberdeen
18	Edinburgh	18	1966
19	72	19	Dundee, Aberdeen, Manchester United and Leeds
20	1997	20	Ardeer
21	1905	21	Sir Patrick Geddes
22	John Maclean	22	1995–97
23	James Connolly	23	George Forrest
24	John Buchan	24	Philosophy
25	Robert Cunninghame Graham	25	George VI

1	St Andrews
2	Portree, Skye
3	Strontian (strontianite, strontium)
4	Dundee
5	Ballater
6	Macpherson
7	Glen Lyon
8	The River Earn
9	Ayr
10	Inverness
11	James Ramsay MacDonald
12	Lerwick
13	Pitlochry
14	Birnam
15	Edinburgh
16	Saltcoats
17	The Moray Firth
18	Fort William
19	Peterhead
20	North Berwick
21	Peebles
22	Gifford (Yester House Estate)
23	Helmsdale
24	Bridge of Allan
25	East Kilbride

1	Drury Street
2	1163
3	1652
4	'Let Glasgow Flourish'
5	Queen Street
6	Pollok Country Park
7	Jail Square
8	1451
9	'Green hollows'
10	George Square
11	1898
12	Glasgow's coat of arms
13	The Barras
14	Trees, plants and ferns. (The Kibble Palace is a glass pavilion in the Botanic Gardens.)
15	Templeton's Carpets
16	Provand's Lordship
17	George Square
18	The Museum of Transport, Kelvin Hall
19	1988
20	Kingston Dock, Queen's Dock and Prince's Dock
21	Castle Street
22	The nineteenth century
23	Victoria Park
24	1990
25	The Citizens Theatre

Around & About in Scotland 3

1 Broughty Ferry
2 A lighthouse near Montrose
3 Craigellachie
4 Islay
5 Seven
6 Glenturret
7 The site of Holyrood Abbey
8 Traquair
9 Wanlockhead
10 Dirleton Castle
11 *Monarch of the Glen* (as Glenbogle Estate)
12 Inchcolm Abbey
13 Kirkcaldy
14 Cupar
15 North Berwick
16 Glasgow
17 Dunfermline
18 Coatbridge
19 South-west
20 The Glasgow Underground
21 Shetland
22 Lathalmond, by Dunfermline
23 The *Harry Potter* series of films
24 The Church of St Athernase
25 Spynie Palace

General Knowledge 20

1 Aberdeen
2 On the Isle of Mull, a tree fossilized by lava
3 Harry Lauder
4 Dumfries and Galloway
5 Glasgow
6 Robert II
7 By Loch Fyne, near Inveraray
8 Powan
9 A cache of Roman silver, dating from the fourth century
10 Edinburgh
11 William Collins
12 Andrew Carnegie
13 Edinburgh
14 Douglas Dunn
15 *A Study in Scarlet*
16 St Mirren
17 Andrew Fletcher of Saltoun
18 The Erskine Hospital
19 The Potato Famine
20 Pottery, Kirkcaldy
21 1990
22 Niel Gow
23 Fraserburgh
24 Orkney
25 A racehorse

ANSWERS

Rivers, Lochs & Falls

1. The Don and the Dee
2. Loch Lochy, Loch Oich and Loch Ness
3. The eighteenth century
4. Loch Ness
5. Loch Lomond
6. Loch Fyne
7. The Nith
8. The Pentland Hills
9. Loch Achray and Loch Katrine
10. The Almond
11. Loch Ericht
12. Eas Coul Aulin, Sutherland
13. Loch Leven
14. The River Garry
15. The River Devon
16. The Falls of Glomach
17. Dunbar
18. 1964
19. The River Spey
20. 'On the bonnie, bonnie banks of Loch Lomond'
21. Tweed's Well
22. The Lowther Hills
23. 65 miles long
24. The River Tay
25. The River Avon

Literature 3

1. The Scottish Highlands
2. Scottish customs, traditions and folklore
3. John Scott Haldane
4. William Sharp
5. The Clearances
6. Tobias Smollett
7. Africa
8. *Travels with a Donkey in the Cevennes*
9. John Wilson
10. Dorothy Dunnett
11. Kenneth Grahame's son Alastair
12. Nigel Tranter
13. The Blackwood Group
14. John Galt
15. A teacher
16. Mary and Jane
17. William Drummond of Hawthornden
18. Arthur Conan Doyle
19. *Stained Radiance*
20. Aberdeenshire
21. *The Wind in the Willows*
22. John Stirling
23. Louise Welsh
24. Edinburgh
25. Aye Write!

ANSWERS

	Whisky		General Knowledge 21
1	The fifteenth century	1	John Balliol and Robert the Bruce
2	1917	2	Four
3	The Scotch Whisky Association	3	Dundee United
4	A Sikes hydrometer	4	California
5	The nineteenth century	5	The Dee
6	By drying the grains	6	Physician
7	A pot still	7	St Johnstone
8	Islay	8	The nineteenth century
9	Orkney	9	Dunkeld Cathedral
10	A mash tun	10	The Clyde Workers Committee
11	Dufftown	11	David McCallum
12	The 1870s	12	355 metres
13	American Prohibition	13	Gordon Strachan
14	A mixture of malt and grain whiskies	14	David Erskine
15	Islay	15	Cliff Hanley
16	Wort	16	Ben Arthur
17	Johnnie Walker	17	The Edinburgh Commonwealth Games
18	Bell's	18	Perth
19	East Lothian	19	Bartholomew
20	Morayshire (Craigellachie)	20	George VI
21	No. The legal definition of Scotch whisky is whisky distilled in Scotland	21	Edinburgh
22	1914	22	'Via Veritas Vita'
23	Producing industrial alcohol	23	Gigha
24	Macallan	24	Andrew Carnegie
25	c) 3 billion	25	Grangemouth

Life & Works of Robert Louis Stevenson

1   Charles Robinson
2   No
3   *An Inland Voyage*
4   A journey across America
5   *The Black Arrow*
6   America
7   Engineering
8   Law
9   1850
10 *Kidnapped*
11 W.E. Henley
12 Edinburgh
13 Tuberculosis
14 A brain haemorrhage
15 *New Arabian Nights*
16 1885
17 1890
18 Fanny Osborne (née Vandegrift)
19 His stepson, Lloyd Osborne
20 The eighteenth century
21 Thomas
22 *Catriona*
23 Isobel
24 1894
25 Professor Sydney Colvin

Great Scots 3

1   David Hume
2   Africa
3   R.D. Laing
4   St Columba
5   Dugald Stewart
6   The Douglas fir
7   Alexander Todd (Baron Todd of Trumpington)
8   Mary, Queen of Scots
9   Andrew Melville
10 The 1860s (1868)
11 William Lorimer
12 He was shot by an unknown assailant.
13 John Napier
14 James Watt
15 Japan
16 Bill McLaren
17 James Adam
18 Robert Barclay
19 Law
20 James IV
21 1702
22 Adam Smith
23 1711
24 Hugh Miller
25 William Roughead

1	1314	1	Iona
2	The English	2	Francis, Lord Jeffrey
3	John Cope	3	Haakon
4	1297	4	Railway locomotives
5	Cumberland	5	The Treaty of London
6	1746	6	The Clan MacGregor
7	John Balliol	7	The nineteenth century
8	Bothwell Bridge	8	The Dundee Shipbuilding Company
9	The Marquis of Montrose	9	Loch Lomond
10	The Battle of Killiecrankie	10	Edinburgh, Holyrood Park
11	Flodden	11	The 1900s
12	Langside	12	c) 67
13	Nechtanesmere	13	Paper making
14	Alnwick	14	Publishing, bookselling
15	William Wallace	15	Oban
16	Otterburn	16	Near Peterhead
17	The Earl of Mar	17	Mary Campbell
18	1263	18	Glasgow
19	Scots	19	Jarlshof
20	James III	20	1666
21	1645	21	Thomas Carlyle
22	Drumclog	22	The 1880s
23	1746	23	The midge
24	1689	24	The Royal Army Service Corps and the RAF
25	Rullion Green	25	Three

ANSWERS

Aberdeenshire, Moray & Highland

1   The West Highland Museum
2   Eight
3   Lochawe
4   Balquhidder churchyard
5   Loch Linnhe
6   Inveraray
7   Scott Skinner
8   Dunrobin Castle
9   Loch Shin
10 It was a spa town.
11 Oldmeldrum
12 Loch Moidart
13 Mallaig
14 Fort Augustus
15 Glencoe
16 Dunnet Head
17 Invergordon
18 The Beinn Eighe National Nature Reserve
19 Osgood Mackenzie
20 Pluscarden Abbey
21 The eighteenth century
22 Fyvie Castle
23 King William III
24 Chanonry Point, near Fortrose
25 Loch Quoich

Perth

1   St John's Kirk
2   Catherine Glover
3   The Salutation Hotel
4   Balhousie Castle
5   Sir Walter Scott (statue)
6   The National Trust for Scotland
7   Pullar
8   1814
9   St Johnstone Football Club
10 1992
11 A new bridge over the River Tay
12 Dewar's Rinks (built on the site of the Dewar's building)
13 St John's Kirk (They are bells.)
14 The nineteenth century
15 1559
16 1967
17 The Battle of the Clans
18 James Smeaton
19 63
20 1911
21 Thomas Anderson and Thomas Hay Marshall
22 George Street
23 1623
24 In the River Tay (It is also known as the Abernethy Pearl.)
25 The Kirkgate

	Mary, Queen of Scots		General Knowledge 23
1	1586	1	Edinburgh
2	Four (one of them twice)	2	Coleridge
3	The Earl of Moray	3	Nigeria
4	The Earls of Maitland and Kirkcaldy	4	Curling
5	She was his great-granddaughter.	5	St Mungo and St Columba
6	Seton, Beaton, Livingston and Fleming	6	Herring fishing
7	Lord James Stewart, Earl of Moray	7	Inverness-shire
8	Archbishop James Hamilton	8	John Stuart Mill
9	Nôtre Dame	9	James Keir Hardie
10	1560	10	Juniper and Scots pine
11	1548	11	Eilean Mor
12	Duke of Albany, King of Scots	12	Robert the Bruce
13	Glasgow	13	The 1960s
14	Duke of Orkney	14	Andrew Carnegie
15	The Earl of Moray	15	The nineteenth century
16	Lady Jean Gordon	16	Nancy
17	Archbishop Hamilton	17	Off the west coast of Mull
18	The Earl of Morton	18	The eighteenth century
19	Carberry Hill	19	Henry
20	To Edinburgh	20	Grangemouth
21	Langside	21	By Perth
22	He was hanged at Stirling.	22	Dundas Vale, Glasgow
23	1570	23	The eighteenth century
24	1573	24	Glenrothes
25	The Earl of Lennox	25	J.M. Barrie

ANSWERS

Inverness

1 Highland Radio
2 Dr Johnson
3 Abertarff House
4 St Andrews Cathedral
5 The nineteenth century
6 King David I
7 The Eden Court Theatre
8 The nineteenth century
9 Montrose
10 Dalcross
11 Corner of Bridge Street and Castle Wynd
12 A stone on which women rested their washing tubs to break the journey carrying water from the river.
13 The nineteenth century
14 Craig Phadrig
15 Sir Alexander Ross
16 The seventeenth century
17 Dominican
18 Bridge Street
19 The sixteenth century
20 St Michael's Mount
21 The eighteenth century
22 The Town House
23 Clava Cairns
24 Culloden Moor
25 The 1840s (1849)

The Romans in Scotland

1 Cramond, Edinburgh
2 The Forth and the Clyde
3 The second century AD
4 Dere Street
5 Trimontium
6 *Circa* AD 80
7 19
8 North of the River Tay
9 Agricola
10 Caledonia
11 Septimus Severus
12 Quintus Lollius Urbicus
13 Banffshire
14 Ardoch
15 AD 84
16 Near Ingliston, Edinburgh
17 Hadrian's Wall
18 The Royal Museum of Scotland, Edinburgh
19 *Circa* AD 140
20 Tacitus
21 AD 84
22 Near Falkirk
23 The A68
24 Vespasian
25 Constantine

ANSWERS

	Heroes & Villains 1		General Knowledge 24
1	John Muir	1	Alloway
2	1305	2	Glenrothes
3	Dunbar Castle	3	The Glasgow Boys
4	He was killed at the Battle of Killiecrankie.	4	The nineteenth century
5	Sir Archibald David Stirling	5	Mount Stuart House, Isle of Bute
6	He was hanged in London.	6	1989
7	Thomas Guthrie	7	Leith
8	Dennis Nilsen	8	Glasgow
9	Matt Busby	9	Tea
10	Sawney Bean	10	The first decade of the twentieth century
11	David Dale	11	Historic Scotland
12	Robert the Bruce	12	Edinburgh
13	Major Thomas Weir of Edinburgh (executed in 1670)	13	Campbeltown Pipe Band
14	Founding Quarrier's Children's Homes	14	Augustinian
		15	The seventh century
15	Peter Manuel	16	Ayrshire
16	Robert Knox	17	David Napier
17	Madeleine Smith	18	St Monans
18	Michael Scott	19	Four
19	Keir Hardie	20	Benedictine
20	He poisoned them.	21	Charles I
21	Aberdeen (Her family moved to Dundee when she was young.)	22	Heriot-Watt University Scottish Borders Campus, Galashiels
22	Eric Liddell	23	The National Trust for Scotland
23	John Smith	24	James V
24	Pringle	25	Loch Lomond and the Trossachs National Park
25	Elsie Inglis		

ANSWERS

Stirling

1   Robert the Bruce
2   William Wallace
3   The Wallace Monument
4   The Chapel Royal, Stirling Castle
5   1967
6   The 1750s
7   The fifteenth century
8   The Castle Wynd
9   William Bruce
10 Broad Street
11 The figure of a unicorn on top of the Mercat Cross
12 The 1st Earl of Stirling
13 Gowan Hill
14 John Cowane's Hospital
15 James VI
16 The seventeenth century
17 A youth hostel
18 James III
19 The Campanile (bell tower)
20 In the castle cemetery
21 The sixteenth century
22 The eleventh century
23 The Smith Art Gallery and Museum
24 The King's Knot
25 St John Street

History 3

1   James VI
2   The Darien Scheme
3   1305
4   1941
5   1941
6   Mungo Park
7   Typhoid
8   Skye
9   1582
10 1651 (Charles II)
11 Malcolm I
12 1822
13 Edinburgh
14 1639
15 Robert Campbell of Glenlyon
16 1306
17 David Leslie
18 Katharine, Duchess of Atholl
19 1586
20 1782
21 c) 1729
22 Through his mother, Marjorie, Countess of Carrick
23 A decorated wooden and metal box (dating from the eighth century)
24 1988
25 Aberdeen

Around & About in Scotland 4

1 Dunfermline
2 Glasgow Harbour and from 2011 at the new Riverside Museum opposite Govan
3 Pictish carvings
4 They are all whisky distilleries
5 Scone Palace
6 The Isle of Mull
7 Maggie Wall
8 Buckie, Findochty, Portknockie
9 Religious martyrs
10 Discovery Point Visitor Centre, Dundee
11 Barry Mill
12 Glen Esk
13 Cardhu
14 Crieff Hydro
15 To the south
16 The Isle of Bute
17 Cliffs
18 Shakespeare's *Hamlet*, starring Mel Gibson (1990)
19 Eaglesham
20 The M9
21 The nineteenth century
22 The Dean Gallery, Edinburgh
23 The eleventh century
24 Robert the Bruce
25 J.M. Barrie

General Knowledge 25

1 Lichen, used for dyeing material
2 The sea eagle
3 Off Shetland
4 A small hamlet
5 Brown and white
6 Fish
7 *The Master of Ballantrae*
8 Field Marshall Lord Kitchener
9 Hamilton
10 Loch Fyne
11 John Brown
12 The Mull of Kintyre
13 Sir Cameron Mackintosh
14 The National Trust for Scotland
15 Robert Kirk
16 1970
17 Abbotsinch
18 Three
19 Robin Oig
20 Sir James Horlicks
21 Bruce family
22 Oor Wullie
23 Celtic
24 Aberlour
25 Lord Braxfield

ANSWERS

Scottish Regiments

1. The Seaforth Highlanders and the Queen's Own Cameron Highlanders
2. The Royal Stewart tartan
3. The Royal Scots Dragoon Guards
4. The Black Watch
5. 1968
6. The Royal Highland Fusiliers (Princess Margaret's Own Glasgow and Ayrshire Regiment)
7. Edinburgh Castle
8. The King's Own Scottish Borderers
9. The north east of Scotland
10. Government tartan
11. 1494
12. The Queen's Own Highlanders
13. The 3rd Carabiniers
14. Fort George
15. The Royal Scots
16. The Argyll and Sutherland Highlanders
17. The King's Own Scottish Borderers
18. Policing the Highlands
19. Cameron of Erracht, Mackenzie of Seaforth
20. Royal Scots Dragoon Guards
21. 2006
22. Thomas Dalyell
23. Perth
24. Hamilton
25. The Scots Guards

Football 2

1. John Greig
2. Five
3. Adam Crozier
4. 1978
5. Aberdeen
6. One
7. 1980
8. Manchester City, Liverpool
9. 2005
10. Jock Stein
11. 1958
12. Willie Ormond
13. Inverness
14. 1972
15. Dundee FC
16. 2004
17. Queen's Park 1958
18. 1975
19. Greenhill Road, Paisley
20. Peru 3, Scotland 1
21. 2004
22. 1885
23. 1970s
24. Dingwall
25. Hibs

ANSWERS

	West & Central Scotland		General Knowledge 26
1	The Cowal Peninsula	1	Arthur Anderson
2	An aqueduct	2	Ayr
3	Cora Linn and Bonnington Linn	3	The second Friday in July
4	'The Cobbler'	4	Stranraer–Larne
5	The island of Arran	5	Kenneth McAlpin
6	Ardrishaig	6	Hamilton
7	Luss	7	Devorguilla
8	The Younger Botanic Garden	8	Dudley D. Watkins
9	Faslane	9	A statue of the Virgin and Child
10	Near Southend in the Mull of Kintyre	10	Montrose
11	Ayr	11	A prison
12	Biggar	12	Cairngorms National Nature Reserve
13	Knapdale Forest in Mid-Argyll	13	1919
14	Glasgow	14	1850
15	Biggar Gasworks Museum	15	Islay
16	Near Paisley	16	Samuel Greig
17	A road (A70) leading from Edinburgh through Carnwath to Lanark	17	The 1820s
		18	Janet Dalrymple
18	The seventeenth century	19	1611
19	Great Cumbrae	20	Berwick
20	Robert II and Robert III	21	Mey Selections
21	Leadhills	22	26 March 2006
22	Kilmarnock	23	Borrowstounness
23	Annick Water, the River Irvine and the River Garnock	24	40 miles
24	Cumnock	25	Barr's Irn-Bru
25	Near Bridge of Weir		

Literature 4

ANSWERS

1. Margaret Oliphant
2. *Coral Island*
3. Glasgow
4. Robert Henryson
5. The 1850s (1859)
6. Edinburgh
7. Richard Hannay
8. Irvine Welsh
9. Neil Gunn
10. Samuel Rutherford Crockett
11. Gavin Maxwell
12. *The Citadel*
13. *Two Men and a Blanket*
14. *Treasure Island*
15. Alasdair Gray
16. Thomas Carlyle
17. Singapore
18. Hugh MacDiarmid
19. Compton Mackenzie
20. Carl MacDougall
21. Lord Auchinleck
22. 1997
23. *The Cutting Room* (2002)
24. Robin Jenkins
25. John MacDougall Hay

Great Scots 4

1. Thomas Carlyle
2. John Leslie
3. James Crichton
4. Alexander Buchan
5. Sir James Frazer
6. Michael Scott
7. *The Edinburgh Review*
8. Geneva
9. *A Treatise of Human Nature* David Hume
10. George Buchanan
11. Thomas Henderson
12. Geology
13. James IV
14. Adam Ferguson
15. Anderson's College, Glasgow
16. Andrew Bell
17. Ulva
18. Aberdeen
19. Anne Grant of Laggan
20. For burning Elgin Cathedral
21. Kenneth Grahame
22. Francis, Lord Jeffrey
23. Henry Stewart, Lord Darnley
24. Hugh MacDiarmid
25. Thomas Reid

ANSWERS

1	Liz Lochhead
2	The 7:84 Theatre Company
3	St Andrews, Fife
4	John Cairney
5	The Royal Lyceum Theatre, Edinburgh
6	Glasgow
7	Hugh MacLennan
8	His Majesty's Theatre
9	Sir David Lindsay
10	Comedy characters created by Rikki Fulton and Jack Milroy
11	Russell Hunter
12	Hector MacMillan
13	Stirling
14	Allan Ramsay
15	Tony Roper
16	The Mull Little Theatre
17	John Byrne
18	Will Fyffe
19	Tom McGrath
20	Edinburgh
21	Rikki Fulton
22	Edinburgh
23	Raindog
24	Sir Kenneth Macmillan
25	Sydney Goodsir Smith

1	Alexander Melville Bell, father of Alexander Graham Bell
2	David Balfour
3	David Mach
4	1962
5	Miss Anne Cruickshank
6	Borthwick Castle
7	The rules of boxing
8	Birch
9	The 1930s
10	Railway locomotives
11	Burns Cottage
12	Melrose Abbey
13	Lady of the Most Ancient and Most Noble Order of the Thistle
14	The Royal Regiment of Scotland
15	Ben Nevis
16	James VI
17	Flyweight
18	1999
19	Aberdeen
20	Deacon Brodie
21	The Average White Band
22	Aberdeen granite
23	The Marquis of Bute
24	Alec Dickson
25	Aberdeen

Clans

1 Niall Og
2 Son of the parson
3 The Borders
4 Dunvegan Castle, Isle of Skye
5 Clan Campbell
6 Mackenzie
7 Campbell of Glenlyon
8 MacDonald
9 Grant
10 Clan Chattan
11 Aberdeenshire
12 Son of Kenneth
13 'Victory or death!'
14 MacDonald
15 Fife
16 'Royal is my race'
17 The Borders
18 Hamiltons
19 Atholl
20 Gordon
21 Kenneth McAlpin
22 The nineteenth century
23 Cameron
24 Clan Donnachie
25 Clan Donald

Medicine in Scotland

1 Sir Alexander Fleming
2 Provost George Drummond
3 John and William Hunter
4 Obstetrics
5 Aberdeen
6 Sir David Bruce
7 Sir William Boog Leishman
8 Sir Patrick Manson
9 Glasgow
10 1867
11 John James Macleod
12 Alan Archibald Campbell Swinton
13 Neuropathology
14 Bone grafts
15 Psychiatry
16 Dunfermline
17 Maternity
18 The Elsie Inglis Hospital
19 Bruntsfield Hospital
20 James Lind
21 The 1860s
22 The 1990s
23 Dugald Baird
24 Robert Liston
25 James Young Simpson

ANSWERS

1. 'Some ha'e meat and canna eat
And some wad eat that want it.
But we ha'e meat and we can eat
And sae the Lord be thankit.'
2. An oatcake
3. Yellow (It is smoked, filleted haddock.)
4. Soft fruit, in particular, raspberries
5. Flour, butter and sugar
6. A fruit very like a raspberry
7. Oatmeal
8. Meal made from scorched oat grains
9. A flat stone upon which an oat bannock would be baked
10. A smoked haddock, smoked in the fishing village of Crail in Fife
11. Nick Nairn
12. Kippers and oysters
13. A spherical, striped mint-flavoured sweet
14. Irn-Bru
15. A Michelin Star
16. Gingerbread
17. Brewing
18. 1985
19. The Belhaven Brewery
20. Tennents
21. Whisky
22. Chips
23. Cheese
24. White Horse
25. A variety of potato

1. Grangemouth
2. Twentieth century
3. Raasay
4. The Clyde
5. 1989
6. Campbeltown Loch
7. Edinburgh
8. Gosford House, by Aberlady
9. The Forties Field
10. The Chambers Encyclopaedia
11. 1993
12. Weavers, at Fenwick, Ayrshire
13. David Muirhead Bone
14. The Blue Blanket
15. Dundee
16. *The New York Herald*
17. Willie Gallagher
18. The Royal Geographical Society
19. The West Coast train (via Carlisle and Glasgow)
20. Methil
21. The Great Upper Clyde Shipbuilders
22. Dunadd Hill
23. Sir Arthur Conan Doyle
24. John Faed
25. The breech-loading rifle

Heroes & Villains 2

1 'Mosquito'
2 John Boyd Orr
3 Deacon Brodie
4 Jock Stein
5 Bible John
6 Hamish MacInnes
7 He was lynched.
8 Sir Alexander Mackenzie
9 William Hare
10 Alexander Selcraig/Selkirk
11 Lord Darnley
12 St Serf
13 William Douglas
14 Rathlin Island
15 Surgeon
16 Cardinal David Beaton
17 Sir James Ross
18 William McGonagall
19 John Smeaton
20 The Sutherland Clearances
21 Sir William Smith
22 Robert MacQueen, Lord Braxfield
23 The development of radar
24 William Wallace
25 Kirkpatrick Macmillan

Life & Works of Robert Burns

1 James MacPherson, hanged in Banff
2 William Burness
3 Auchamore, by Dunoon
4 21
5 Mrs Robert Cumming (Lesley Baillie)
6 Lochlea
7 John Davidson
8 Ellisland
9 1796
10 1784
11 His sister
12 His son, William
13 William Fisher
14 R. (Robert) Aitken, Esq.
15 Charlotte Stewart, daughter of Bonnie Prince Charlie
16 Greenock
17 William Peebles
18 Agnes Brown
19 Jamaica
20 As an excise officer
21 Elizabeth Paton
22 1790
23 17867
24 *Scots Musical Museum*
25 Mossgiel

ANSWERS

	Scotland's Coastline		General Knowledge 29
1	St Monans	1	The Turnpike Trusts
2	The Firth of Forth	2	Dundee
3	Kirkcudbright	3	The 1880s
4	Wigtown Bay	4	Henry VIII
5	Eyemouth	5	The Declaration of Arbroath
6	Ayr	6	Oyne, near Insch
7	Eigg	7	Dumbarton
8	Loch Broom	8	Partick Thistle
9	Spey Bay	9	Dirleton
10	Scalasaig	10	*Heart of Midlothian*
11	The Bell Rock Lighthouse	11	Thread
12	The Sound of Raasay	12	A reaping machine
13	The Firth of Lorn	13	Malcolm III
14	Dalmeny	14	David Octavius Hill
15	Morar	15	Isobel Johnstone
16	Montrose	16	Chemist
17	Ailsa Craig	17	Enric Miralles
18	South Queensferry	18	Adam Smith
19	Tantallon Castle	19	The Scottish National Party
20	Catterline	20	Graeme Souness
21	Lighthouses	21	William Symington
22	Turnberry Castle	22	George Walton
23	Aberlady Bay	23	Glasgow
24	Kirkcudbright	24	1846
25	North Berwick Law	25	July

ANSWERS

Mountains & Hills

1. Loch Maree
2. A mountain over 3,000 feet in height
3. Braeriach (4,252 feet)
4. Kintail
5. Ben Ledi
6. Lochnagar
7. 4,409 ft
8. Arran
9. Ben MacDui
10. The Campsie Fells
11. Ben Hope
12. Beside Loch Earn
13. Big Hill
14. Loch Tay
15. Suilven
16. The Cairngorms
17. The Grampians
18. Ben MacDui (4,295 feet)
19. Sgurr Alasdair
20. The Great Glen
21. Schiehallion
22. Drumochter Pass
23. A mountain between 2,500 and 3,000 feet high
24. Easter Ross
25. The Great Shepherd of Etive

History 4

1. Lord Lovat
2. Donald Dewar
3. Scone
4. 1565
5. Patrick Hamilton
6. 1266
7. 1411
8. 1650
9. Robert II
10. George Wishart
11. 1973
12. James V
13. 1560
14. Malcolm IV
15. John Balliol
16. David II
17. The fifteenth century
18. 1996
19. Malcolm III
20. The 250th anniversary of the Battle of Culloden
21. Malcolm III and William the Conqueror
22. The Alien Act
23. Edward Balliol
24. A black bull's head
25. 1539

	Holy People & Holy Places 2			General Knowledge 30

1 George MacLeod

2 Blantyre

3 Ellary, Argyll

4 The United Presbyterian Church, St Vincent Street

5 St Salvator's College, St Andrews

6 The sixth century

7 1617

8 St Mirren

9 Eigg

10 St Brendan

11 Greece

12 St Martin of Tours

13 Alan Archibald Campbell Tait

14 St Thenew

15 Bishop Richard Holloway

16 St Cuthbert

17 St Leonard

18 Sir Basil Spence

19 Adamnan

20 Mary Levison

21 The twelfth century

22 Dornoch Cathedral

23 The eighth century

24 Farne Island

25 The 1980s

---

1 The 1970s (1977)

2 2 April

3 Jason White

4 In the port of Leith, Edinburgh

5 Two

6 Borthwick Castle

7 As a cure for rheumatism

8 A prison

9 The Younger Botanic Garden

10 Aberdour House

11 Orkney

12 John Logie Baird

13 Gigha

14 Thomas Muir

15 The Kailyard School

16 India

17 Iona

18 William Low

19 Loch Tay

20 Sir Nicholas Fairbairn

21 Berwickshire

22 Buckie

23 Cistercian

24 Inns built on the military roads constructed in Scotland

25 A poet

ANSWERS

Wildlife 2

1 The adder
2 The pine marten
3 Giant hogweed
4 St Kilda
5 The wildcat
6 Balranald
7 The Bass Rock
8 The Flow Country, Caithness and Sutherland
9 St Kilda
10 The Highlands, particularly in pine forest
11 Purple (with a yellow eye)
12 Caithness, Orkney and Shetland
13 The islands of Mull and Skye
14 The sea eagle
15 The white-tailed eagle
16 The great black-backed gull
17 The tenth century
18 The puffin
19 The gannet
20 Near Stonehaven
21 St Kilda
22 The Sands of Forvie
23 A great skua
24 Beinn Eighe
25 The grey seal

Myth & Mystery, Magic & Superstition 2

1 Glamis Castle
2 A poltergeist
3 A dish of salt
4 A healthy, fine-looking stalk and leaves meant a healthy, handsome husband (and a poor-looking one, the opposite). The amount of earth left on the root indicated the wealth her future husband would have.
5 It was believed to cause the child to become a thief.
6 It is inviting death into the house.
7 Thomas the Rhymer
8 Greyfriars Kirkyard, Edinburgh
9 Fingal (Fionn)
10 '. . . 'til May is oot.'
11 If the person was indeed the murderer, it was believed that the corpse would bleed
12 The ghost of a monk
13 '. . . Deil's luck.'
14 Imminent death in the vicinity
15 A mark on a woman's skin which identified her as a witch. If a pin was plunged into the mark, it would not bleed.
16 The Battle of Pinkie
17 The sixteenth century
18 Pebbles on the beach
19 To allow the dead person's soul a clear flight
20 It was thought to bring about the early death of the child who was normally the occupant.
21 Mary of Guise
22 Ben MacDui
23 Mary King's Close
24 The ghost of a sailor
25 Glamis Castle